BOAT. RIVER. PERSON.

AWAKENESS

a state of being awake and fully aware in the
present moment—alive, aliveness

What's awakeness got to do with it?

In this inspiring book, the author takes us on a journey that invites us to understand and wake up to our true Self. For most of us, that deep and wise part of us is often asleep. While we sleep, the "river" of our lives can buffet, toss and ground our "boat" onto islands of unhappiness and failure.

BOAT. RIVER. PERSON. brings hope to marooned people, relationships and sex lives.

Through stories from her life and therapy sessions, she introduces new ways of talking about relationships and sex, like "Thinking about Thinking" or "I Count—You Count", and practical exercises like "Knee to Knee". This book wakes you up to your own wisdom and contentment.

BOAT.
RIVER.
PERSON.

Journeys to Awakeness in
Life, Relationships, and Sex

Sensovi Press

Lisa Terrell

Illustrations by JJ Richards
Author photo by Carrie Allen
Cover layout and book design by Spiro Books

All the clients referenced in this book are fictional composites of common cases the author works with.

First edition 2023

Manufactured in the United States of America
25 24 23 22 21 20 19 18 17 1 2 3 4 5

ISBN 979-8-9890249-1-9 (hardcover)
ISBN 979-8-9890249-0-2 (paperback)
ISBN 979-8-9890249-2-6 (eBook}

Author's Note

I'm glad Oprah doesn't have a daily TV show anymore.

In the years I have worked on this book, I have hoped it would help people, perhaps a lot of people. But not too many. Not so many that Oprah's people might call me to come talk about my sex book. Because, you know—sex! On TV. On YouTube. Millions of views. The introverted part of me gets nervous at just the thought of that.

This is a sex book, and it isn't a sex book.

It is true that I am a sex therapist. It is true that I work with people who want to work on their sex lives. And it's complicated.

I have these ideas about sex, happiness, intimacy, and meaning. Rather than satisfaction and happiness, I propose meaning and Contentment. Rather than being a good person, doing your best, and keeping yourself desirable, I suggest finding your Self. Find your Self. Live from the awareness that Self provides. Not the story of yourself.

See, it's complicated.

I think the word "self" tends to be boring. Especially compared to a word like sex. Like a wall painted a beige color, you don't notice the word "self." At least, not like you would notice a deep-red wall. That's how people react to the word "sex." Sex immediately draws attention. It seems to me that in our world of 280 characters including spaces, going viral, and our Borg-like phone Collective, the ideas of Self are like throwing a cup of water into the ocean!

Still, I'm not sure I could say no to Oprah!

Who knows all the sex-related things people will be searching for when this book pops up in a link? "Low desire," "help with intimacy," "satisfaction," or some slangy word like "hard." And yes, "how to turn someone on." And, of course, "sex."

I guess that's okay. Yet this is more than a sex book.

Another worry is that this will be called a self-help book. Yes, it would feel great to walk into a Barnes and Noble or Books-a-Million and see my book on the shelves, hanging out with the other books like a normal book. Yet the category "self-help" feels like it minimizes the book. I know quite a large number of people who won't pick up a self-help book and have no interest in a self-help app or website.

There's nothing for it. Technically, this is a self-help book.

Yet I wonder, could I call it a "Self-find" book? A book to help you find your "Self?"

That is my intention. To help the reader connect with their "Inner Self." Their truest "Self." Their deepest "Self." And as I call it in this book, their Inner Person Self.

In my experience, the stories people tell themselves about their self are what keep them stuck. I have seen that often it is what causes the problem in the first place. Especially in intimacy and sex.

I want to tell you about this Self[1] thing. If you look at all your relationships and your Sexuality, you can locate your Self. Not the "story of your self." "Your Self." In the process of working on your relationships, your dating life, or your sex life, you can discover and understand your real you.

So, whether this is a sex book, a self-help book, or something else, my highest hope for this book is that those who pick it up will experience it as an invitation.

You. I invite you.

This is your invitation for you to find and explore the deepest part of you. Let's go farther than you have ever gone to find that deepest wisdom within yourself.

The deep "you" that knows how to find your way.

Consider yourself invited.

---

1 Throughout this book the word self is capitalized to represent the concept of Inner Person Self. The word self without the capital indicates a general reference to you or your understanding of your Outer Self. See the Concept Guide in the Appendices for more working definitions and words that are capitalized to indicate a specific definition.

Contents

Appendices

Introduction : Contentment

This book is about Contentment, or, more precisely, how to experience and practice more Contentment more often.

Not the not-resting kind of contentment that says, "I'm not going to be content until I've got what I want."

Not the worried-you-are-settling-for-less-than-you-should kind of contentment that says, "I'm not going to be content with this. I won't settle for this."

Neither of those.

The kind of Contentment I'm talking about is like the children's story where Goldilocks went looking for the chair, the porridge, and the bed that were "just right." It is a sense of peace that you feel inside of you. It's when our body, mind, and the part of us that feels the body and hears the thoughts of our mind—our Self—all feel peaceful. Mind. Body. Self. Content.

My work as a clinical counselor is about helping people who are not content find and practice Contentment. I see it as a journey that we are all on. We can use the things in our lives that are not going well to help us understand ourselves and keep moving to a better place. A place that is just right for us.

I want to give you some ideas about the journey to Contentment that I think will help you. These ideas are straight from my relationship and sexuality work and are continually refined by the wisdom that each client brings to the work. This book enables me to walk with you for a while and share what I have learned. The three major ideas I am excited to share with you are how to "practice" Contentment, The Five Views of Self, and a very special painting that provides a profound metaphor about Self.

So, who is this book for? It is for anyone who wants to feel Contentment on the inside.

- The single person who doesn't want to be single
- The person who secretly feels they are not in the right relationship for them

1

- The couple struggling to be happy together
- The couple arguing over sex
- The person who feels like they aren't sexual
- The person who keeps losing their temper and rages
- The person who is ashamed of their body
- The person who feels betrayed by their body because it is not cooperating with them
- The person who doesn't trust their partner
- The person who struggles with anxiety or depression
- The person who struggles with addiction
- The person who doesn't know why they act the way they do
- The person struggling with memories that keep popping back up on replay

This Contentment journey is one that every human is invited to. It is a journey to understand yourself and learn to wake up to your fullest life possible.

This book is divided into three sections that describe the three steps to getting to Contentment.

Section 1 is "What if?" We all have stories about what we know and what we don't. Asking "What if?" or paying attention to our "wake-up moments" and "Ahas" is the place to start. "What if" helps us find "what we don't know we don't know."

Section 2 is "What Is?"/What Is This is coming into the present moment. It is not a story of who we are. It is the place where our wise Self is awake and able to be in the moment. Assisted by your Mind and Body, you are able to do what you want and need to do. You wake up by finding and being in What Is.

Section 3 is "Awakeness" Being awake is living your life from your wise Inside Self. This section is about how to practice waking up, staying awake, and waking up more often. To guide you on your journey, I will help you examine your story—stories—that you tell yourself about yourself.

The second thing I will share in this book is my trusty "map." It is the map I have used many times in my therapy work to alleviate pain and suffering in relationships and sexuality. It is a map of the Five Stories of Self. You may not speak your stories out loud, but they are there and they are what you follow as you live your life day to day. Each of the five types of stories are the paths we follow to understand ourselves.

I want to help you find your "You are Here" star—to help you find and understand your real You. When you find your Self, you wake up. Waking up is the skill you will need to practice Contentment.

It is a journey each human takes. We may not realize it. We may at times get stuck or turn back on our journey. But we always, always have our Self right there waiting for us.

You will see the **Five Views of Self**, five ways of understanding our Self, throughout this book:

- **Latent Self**
- **Performance Self**
- **Validation Self**
- **Responsive Self**
- **Integrated Self**

The first three views of Self come from stories about ourselves that come from outside of us. They are our Outside Self.

Latent Self Stories are about how we fit into our world.

The Latent Self is where we understand our self and act from the viewpoints from our Self of Origin. The Self of Origin includes the Self we were as a baby and the life we were and are surrounded by. Our upbringing, our responses to that upbringing, and our stories about life all become a part of us. Our understanding of who we are comes from our origin story. Mother, father, sister, brother, orphan, only child, happy, not happy, rules, secrets—lots of things create our story of origin. As we become adults, we add to the sense of where we came from. Our understanding of ourselves is based on "who we are," where we belong, what roles we fulfill, where we are safe and comfortable, where we have our life, our environment, our culture.

Performance Self Stories are about how well we meet expectations and goals.

The Performance Self is our scorecard of how we are doing as a human. We begin adding to our story of origin. We add evaluations based on aspirations of who we want to be, expectations from ourself and others, comparisons to others. At this stage of the journey, we may have numerous stories about how we are faring, how well we are meeting our goals for our self. We understand who we are; our self is based on how we are doing compared to our expectations and compared to what others expect of us.

3

Validation Self Stories are about how others see us.

The Validation Self is when we look around to get love, approval, and worthiness from other people. We understand who we are based on what others validate, approve of, and give the thumbs up to.

When we are using the stories, the paths of Latent, Performance, or Validation, we are focused on our life as it is lived outside, what is coming at us from our daily lives.

Meanwhile, we are missing something very important. Our Self is missing. Well, not really missing, but sound asleep.

We think that we are awake. We have all these thoughts, voices, and images in our heads all the time. Isn't that awake? No. All of those thoughts, voices, and images are a river that never stops. This River is a part of you, but it is not your Inner Self—you. Your mind and your "Self" are two separate parts of you.

Let's try that out. Right this moment, think about what you are thinking. What are the thoughts that you notice? You may want to jot them down. Write down your exact words that are floating by.

Now, let's check. Who is the one who saw those thoughts? When you step back to think about thinking, it is your Inner Person Self who is able to step back from your thoughts and jot them down.

This is how you begin the next part of the journey. You work to see and understand your Self. Not the stories of the Latent Self. Not how well you are doing in parts of your life—your Performance Self. Not what any other person in this world thinks or says (Validation Self) you are. Your Self is the inside you, the part of you that can think about thinking and know and understand your body. That's the real you, your Self.

The next part of the journey is very exciting. It's the part where you begin to wake up from inside of you, where the view of your "self" changes to looking at your experiences of your "Self." You begin to find the information that is inside you. You start understanding the "real story of you." You practice being Responsive and Integrated. These are your Inside Self experiences, your truth.

Responsive Self Truth comes from our own wisdom. The Responsive Self is when we start looking around inside of ourselves. We start thinking about thinking. We notice our inner space. We notice our Body by checking for sensations, energy levels, and what our Body is communicating to us. We consult our Body to see what it has to say about what our Mind is going on about.

Who is this we? It is our Inner Person Self. We become more awake and present in our life.

Integrated Self

We bring our actual experiences and understandings of Inner Self, our truth, to our day-to-day life and relationships, and we invite others to do the same. The Integrated Self is when we are skillful at being awake and present when other people are around. We practice watching our minds and check with our body to be fully awake and alive. As we practice and become more skillful at including our Self (not the story of self), we are able to hold onto ourselves and our experience while paying attention to and experiencing another person. We practice including our Inner Person Self in our relationships while paying fuller attention to others' experiences and we invite others to do the same.

The Responsive and Integrated parts of the journey happen inside us. For all of us, it starts on the Outside and goes In. Although we can't be perfectly and completely Responsive and Integrated, we learn to use our wisdom gleaned from our What Is to guide and calibrate our actions. We learn what to do when the world around us and our relationships are chaotic and <u>not</u> integrated.

We will know we are on the right track, that we are making progress, when we begin to be able to rest in the moment. We are able to rest because we are beginning to understand that we are okay, lovable, of great worth, and our life is of highest value. We will be more ourselves when we start to learn how to make peace inside us. When we become more awake and alive in our day-to-day life, we will understand and feel Contentment.[1]

And last but not least, I want to share a special painting with you. An expressionist type of painting in beautiful colors, it skillfully portrays a picture of a person in a boat who is awake and paddling their boat where they want to go. It is a great metaphor to keep in your memory, a reminder of how to stay awake and alive in your life. It is an awake person in a boat on a river.

As we explore this metaphor, the Boat represents your Body. Boat Body. The River represents your Mind. River Mind. The Person in the Boat on the River represents our Inner Person Self. More specifically, we look to see if the Person is asleep and taking the ride wherever the River takes the Boat, or if the Person is awake. Being awake means you can watch the thoughts in the River and check

---

1   You will notice the word Contentment and many concept words are capitalized in this book. The capitals are to alert you that a word is important. It indicates the word is part of the process related to the Journey of Contentment, or a word for which I use a very specific definition in order to distinguish it from vernacular or slang usage. For a list of important words and their definitions, see the Concept Guide in the Appendices.

in with how the Boat is doing to make wise choices. Awake people paddle their way to Contentment.

This is quite the journey. For most of us, it will take a long time. It is my hope that my guidance here will be a profound help on your journey to Contentment.

Depression, anxiety, failing or failed relationships, shame, guilt, lousy sex, no sex, loss, rejection, or unrealized dreams or goals might be the way we start our journey. We could also start our journey when something really good happens that gets us paying attention to our Outside Self compared to our Inner Self. How we start the journey isn't important.

Begin where you are.

WHAT IF?

Start with "What if?"

"What if?" is a key that opens the door to what you don't know you don't know. It's not always easy to ask "What if?"

This introductory section has two parts. Part One introduces you to how we all tend to live our lives going with the flow of our minds in response to our day-to-day situations. We live with a focus on our Outside Self. Through Aha's, distress, wake-up moments, and ordinary days we have the opportunity to ask "What if?" and enable ourselves to start thinking about things we didn't know we didn't know.

In Part Two I share a time in my life when I ignored my truth and was completely immersed in Outside stories about myself. I was adrift and it caused my Boat Body to take drastic measures to get my attention. It was a special painting of a boat, river, and person in the boat that helped me go from my Outside Self to waking up and understanding my Inner Person Self and the wisdom that was already there.

PART ONE

Unknown Places

Welcome to Sex Therapy

It is almost 1 p.m. I get a new client chart, fill my water mug, and freshen my lipstick.

I go down the wooden stairs of the early 1900s–era house where I have my office. The clomp-clomp of my shoes announces to those in the waiting area that I am on my way. Rounding the corner, I meet Marc and Kiersten. Even with the noisy advance notice, both look surprised to see me.

"Hello, I'm Dr. Lisa Terrell. You must be Marc and Kiersten?"

They both nod, and Kiersten says, "It has been so stressful to get here!"

Marc had the appointment down as 2 p.m. Kiersten had called him at the last minute to say that the email said 1 p.m. They did arrive a few minutes early only to realize they didn't know the door code to get into the waiting area. There was a hurried trip back to the car to get the phone that had the code.

"Even through all that, you have arrived on time!" I compliment. I deliberately slow my words and look each in the eyes as I smile to reassure them. I got this.

We all go back up the stairs into my office and settle into the oversized leather chairs.

Marc and Kiersten have officially begun sex therapy.

*   *   *

I always feel uneasy with these beginning sessions. I know that I will be leading them to a place they don't know that they don't know yet. It will take courage, theirs and mine. Not everyone is ready for the journey.

15

Clients coming to sex therapy are often beyond uneasy. It's hard to come to that first session. They worry that they may be told they aren't a good fit for each other. They worry that they will feel humiliated when they share what has happened to them. They feel embarrassed just having to be here in this office with me. They wonder if I will tell them to do things that they just don't want to do or are unable to do.

I get it.

It takes courage to come and tolerate the discomfort of that first session—a journey to an unknown place.

I stay focused. I am their guide. They are depending on me to show them how to get unstuck and continue their journey.

I know that most of my clients will be relieved and glad that they had been so unhappy in their sex life that they came to sex therapy.

The first goal is to help Marc and Kiersten practice something that they will learn to do for themselves. From the first session, I will help them with what I already know is missing. From the very first session, I will take them to their Sexuality to find it.

Their Sexuality is like a book of stories they have collected about sex. Each story in the book tells about how they see and understand their Self.

I will show them what their stories of sex are doing to them. To be content in their sex life together they will need to find the missing part in their sexual experiences. They can learn the process of waking up and becoming Responsive to self. In turn, this allows a person to invite and meet their partner's Self.

The walk up the stairway to enter sex therapy begins a journey into Sexuality that is surprising for many. They come to fix their sex life. We will likely reset their sex life for the better and in the process help them take a deep personal journey.

To put it simply, if sex isn't going well, it's because of the story you have about sex. I know that if you are ready and willing, your sex stories will always tell you where you are at and what you need to do.

I have no doubt that if they begin to understand what their Sexuality is telling them about their Self, they will know what to do. They will make a change. But for now, I need to prepare them for the journey.

I start with a pretend-not-pretend question. "What would you tell a trusted friend about this relationship? If your friend asked how it feels to be married, what would you tell them?"

Marc starts. "It is work at times, but I would tell friends it is so worth it. I love Kiersten. It just makes me so upset when she tells me she feels like I am not attracted to her. I try to tell her that I'm still very attracted to her. She is so beautiful to me. I try to tell her how nervous I get. Especially when it has been a while since we have had intimacy."

I break in, "What do you mean by intimacy?"

With a bit of hesitation, he quietly says, "Sex."

I invite him to continue.

"I'll start thinking about it, and as I think about it, I will feel more and more worked up. So by the time I get home, I almost talk myself out of trying to have sex."

"What do you mean worked up?" I ask.

"I keep thinking, 'What if I can't perform?' Then Kiersten is going to get upset, thinking that I don't desire her. Yet if I don't try to have sex, she's going to think I don't desire her."

I notice the word "perform," but save my thought for later. "So, you are worrying a lot about sex?"

"Yah, I think about it every day, and if I think Kiersten will want to have sex, I really get jammed up."

I invite him to continue. "What have you tried to help with this erection problem?"

"I've been trying lots of stuff. I saw my doctor and got my testosterone tested."

These interruptions to check the meanings of the words are not bad manners; they serve an important purpose. These first questions and answers are important for history-taking, but even more important than the history is that from our first session, I begin to prepare them to see what they don't know they don't know. I want to know what the words mean to Marc, and I want Marc to tune in to what they mean. What does it mean to him to perform? What does intimacy mean to him? What does desire mean? What is Marc and Kiersten's story of sex?

Checking the meanings of the words with clients is a way to guide the conversation to Sexuality. I stay very encouraging, but guide the conversation carefully on the path to what they don't know.

I guide Marc and Kiersten deeper into sacred ground. This is not just shooting the breeze; this is Process Therapy. I work to help each one find words to tell me about their experience. What do "libido," "desire," and "sex" mean to them? Again and again, I help them identify the difference between sexual slang and what they actually experience in negotiating and meeting their partner during sex. I want to know what they "know," because their new sex life is waiting for them in what they don't know that they don't know.

I summarize Marc's answer to the pretend-not-pretend question. "So, you feel good about your marriage, but you are very worried that this sexual problem might be serious. Is that right?"

Marc nods in agreement.

I turn to Kiersten. "What would be your summary of the relationship?"

"We have had our ups and downs, but I always know we love each other. We have the same goals and values. Sex has always been an issue for us. I have always felt like I am more sexual than Marc."

I focus on Kiersten now. "What does 'more sexual' mean to you?"

"It has been a long time since Marc has initiated sex. At the beginning of our relationship, he would sometimes initiate, but always in the same way and the same time. When we were in bed, the lights out, and ready to go to sleep."

"You are the one who usually initiates?"

"Yes. I've always been the one to try to talk about our sex life. And it seems if I didn't push for it, we would go months without having sex. I'm worried how we are going to get anything out of this therapy. Just like coming today. If I hadn't checked up on Marc, he would have missed the session. I have been begging him and begging him to come to sex therapy. I feel like he doesn't care. I feel like he doesn't want me."

"How would you know he wants you?"

"If he initiated sex and could perform."

I don't let the word get by this time. "What do you mean by 'perform'?"

Kiersten answers without hesitation, "To have and keep his erection."

This is an obvious place for the couple of not knowing what they don't know they don't know. Everything depends on Marc's erection. They don't negotiate, and they don't meet their partner. I take note of this for later. It would do little good to point this out at this moment.

I invite Marc back into the conversation by asking him the next question. "What do you hope to get out of sex therapy?"

Marc says, "I know Kiersten wants more intimacy—more sex," he self-corrects. (This is good. He is in Sexuality territory!) "I've just had a struggle with my libido since I started taking depression medication."

I ask "What does the word libido mean to you?"

"You know, wanting to have sex," he says.

"How would you know you wanted to have sex?"

"I could get an erection. I always had some times when I would struggle with my erections, but it has gotten a lot worse since the medication. I did go to the doctor and he checked my testosterone. My levels were normal. He did give me a prescription for Cialis. I would like our sex life to go back to the way it was. It used to be easy; I didn't give it a thought. Now I get stressed even if I know we will have an opportunity or if Kiersten touches me affectionately."

Kiersten chimes in. "I have now started to be hesitant to touch him because I can feel him tense up and move away from me. I don't think he desires me."

"How would you know he desired you?" I ask.

"We don't have intimacy—sex [she also self-corrects]—for weeks on end. I think that if he desired me, he would want to have sex."

Marc shakes his head. "I've tried to tell her that I am attracted to her—but I can see how it hurts her when this happens."

My next question is to check out what I already suspect.

"How do you invite each other to have sex?"

Looking at each other, they take turns telling about how they start sex.

They begin to be touchier with each other. They kiss. Both of them know the signals and try to figure out if they are a "go" to have sex. One person can ignore and move away from the other if they don't want to try sex. It's a language that this couple understands well and it actually works pretty well. It sends the "No, I don't want to have sex" signal and it sends the "Yes, I'm willing to have sex" signal.

At least that's the way they used to start sex. The usual way of getting together to have sex has now been shortened.

"So, now the only thing it takes to proceed to sex is an erection?" I ask.

They both say, "Yes."

"So, it doesn't matter what has been going on with your day, if you get the signal from your partner, you may be willing to have sex? So, you don't really talk, you just start moving to each other?"

They both nod in agreement.

As Marc and Kiersten continue to talk, it is confirmed for me that they do not experience each other when trying to have sex. They don't talk, they start to kiss, and they both are watching to see if Marc gets an erection.

19

They are going by what they "know"—the story of sex. The story is if you desire your partner, you will be aroused and you will stay aroused. Therefore, having an erection means you have desire for your partner. If there isn't an erection, it means something is broken.

Marc and Kiersten feel very broken. As erections have become more and more absent, their story of sex has beaten up their sense of self.

They worry their broken sex life means their couple's story may be over. I assure them it isn't.

I know their story is just getting to the good part.

Just Getting to the Good Part
When Life Isn't Working, Look for the Unexpected

At the end of my first session with Marc and Kiersten, I said they were just getting to the good part.

Now you may be asking if you aren't feeling good about your sex life, how is that getting to the good part? The answer is that the problem, the pain, and the discomfort are what help you be willing to journey to a new and unknown place. When you have something happen that doesn't feel good, ask "What if?" The process of asking the "What if?" helps you begin to question your story and wake up your Self.

Your stories tell you what you know and what you don't know. "What if?" helps you find what you don't know you don't know.

It might be helpful if I tell you about the first few times I went to a hot yoga class. My yoga practice has taught me an important thing for my life and for my sex therapy work.

I remember halfway into my first hot yoga class I heard the life-changing "What if?" in the form of guidance from the teacher.

I was very miserable at 103 degrees, 39.4 Celsius. I was sweating and dizzy, wondering how I was going to make it through class.

"I hate this!" I shouted silently.

As I watched the slender young lady next to me smoothly move into "standing bow pose" in perfect time with the muscly guy in front of her, I thought, "I'm never going to be able to do that!"

As usual with exercise, I went back to my usual story about myself. "I shouldn't eat so much, that's why I am so heavy! These people don't overeat like me."

I was struggling to keep up with the teacher's cues when he said, "If you are dizzy, you are doing it right!"

"What?" I remember pausing and thinking. "This does not feel good!"

I soon learned the reason why dizziness was a good sign. Some of the poses are specifically meant to raise your heart rate! I learned that at the very moment I was about to fall over, I actually was on the right track. My heart was getting a workout.

After some time, as I "woke up" in yoga, I realized it wasn't a yes-or-no activity. It wasn't "Yes, I am doing yoga right" or "No, I am not doing yoga right." It wasn't "I can do this pose" or "I cannot do this pose," or "Wow, I'm doing this pose all wrong!" or "Wow, I'm nailing it!"

My job in yoga, how to do yoga "right," was to stay with myself. To pay attention to my What Is—my experience.

Up to that point, I was doing yoga with a running inner conversation. I was going through all the stories about the heat, the poses, the other people in class, my belly.

In order to leave my stories and get to my What Is—my experience—I had to challenge the "either or" of "you can do yoga" or "you can't do yoga." I had to ask the "What if?" about doing yoga. "What if" it wasn't about doing it right or wrong, but about staying awake to the What Is of what I am experiencing in this moment?"

I began to learn to tune in to my body to pick up on my body messages much earlier, to pace myself not according to the stories, but to what my body was communicating to me. I started to get through class with much more ease.

Those surprising words helped me find my real experience, my "What Is," as I practiced yoga. That new way, that "What if?" about my struggle, kept me in the room and brought me back to many more classes.

"What if?" is a powerful question.

When life is kicking you in the butt—you feel miserable, beyond hope, or beaten down—start asking it. "What if?" moves you out of the "yes or no, either or" way of thinking and knowing.

We must find a way to ask it, because it will take us to where we don't know we don't know. It's the "good part!"

Sometimes we are blessed with an "Aha!" An Aha is a moment when the "What if?" comes to us without us asking. The events of our life give opportunity to move out of the stories we tell ourselves, into what we actually experience.

Birth. Loss. Death. Crisis. Pain. Joy. Reverses in fortune. Certain people who come into our life. Each event or person is a teacher inviting us to ask "What if?"

I still enjoy hot yoga today, where water breaks are "party time" and checking in with yourself to see how you and your body are doing is how you "do it right."

It's not so different in your life.

A surprising part of counseling is the idea that if things aren't going well, it might be a good sign. Rather than meaning your relationship or marriage isn't going to make it, it can mean your partnership is ready to grow. Rather than meaning your sex life is messed up and broken, it can mean you are ready for the next thing. Sex therapy is an opportunity to check in with yourself to honestly see how you *and* your body are doing. That's how you do it right.

That's why I often say, "If you find yourself unhappy with your sex life, be glad!" "If your partner is unhappy with your sex life, throw a party!" "If your relationship is in chaos, be glad!"

Well, I don't actually say that to many people, but it is how I think about it. When life isn't going well, it is a signal: it is an opportunity to see the "What if?"

I know it doesn't feel good. You feel embarrassed, broken, frustrated, and cheated. "Why can't I be like other people?" I hear you. It sucks. But I assure you there is a big reveal waiting to happen in your troubles.

It's something to take note of. It's a helpful message. It's useful information. It is a cause for celebration. Really. This is good.

If you feel miserable in your relationship, what if it is as if your relationship has had an awkward "growth spurt" and now none of the usual "clothes" fit?

If sex isn't as easy as it used to be, or is disappointing, and often makes you feel unsettled or you sometimes fall into despair—you are likely doing it right. The disappointment is a signal of what to pay attention to. Your life is on track. Woohoo!

Not having sex? You also are doing it right!

If you aren't "unhappy" with sex, and come from more of a place that you really want to keep a good thing going—perfect!

That will work! It's time for you, too.

Does that sound too cheerful? Do you think I just don't understand?

I assure you—I get it. I help people with their relationships and sex lives. Frustrated people. Unhappy people. Depressed and anxious people. People who are completely at the end of their rope with their partner. With sex. With not having sex.

You may ask "If I'm doing it right, why is it so hard? Why do I feel so miserable in this relationship? Why does my sex life suck?"

It's so hard because of your story. Your story is what you "know." The thing about our stories is they may be misleading us to think that we are a certain way, that our situation is a certain way, when the real story—the truth, the reality, the experience—is different.

In my story of starting hot yoga, I was clear about what I knew. I went in knowing that I didn't know how to do hot yoga. Sure enough, as class began it was clear that I didn't know how to do this yoga. I knew that I wasn't keeping up and that it would be hard to keep up. I thought, "This is too hard!" That first twenty minutes, my story was about whether I would be able to do this class and enjoy it. It was a "yes or no" story. And I was convinced it was "no" very quickly.

The turning point in that yoga class was when the instructor gave me my "What if?" thought. The "What if?" challenged my story. The "What if?" statement of "If you are dizzy and feeling too hot, you are doing it right." The "What if?" helped me to understand that I didn't know what I didn't know. I thought I knew what I didn't know, and I did—kind of. But it wasn't until I was willing to look at the story I had about starting hot yoga that I was able to access the real story. The good part.

What if I was doing it right? This moved me from "Can you do this yoga? Yes or no?" or "Do you like this yoga? Yes or no?" My either or turned to including both and using the word "and." "This yoga makes me feel dizzy and hot *and* I am doing it right!" By acknowledging and paying attention to my body's messages, I already knew how to do this yoga. It no longer was a "yes or no" story. By asking the "What if?" I was able to move to "both and" thinking, and my real experience and my wisdom.

I would bet that you have "yes or no, either or" stories. "Yes or no" stories are based on what you know, what you are telling yourself about you in your relationship and/or your sex life. What you "know" about your partner. What you "know" about sex. You know sex shouldn't be this way. You know you could be, need to be, want to be, should want to be having sex.

Think about this. Have you ever been going along having a pretty good day when an inconvenience interrupted your good day? A friend doesn't show up for your lunch date. Doubts about the friendship pop into your mind. "They are careless, they don't put things in their calendar."

You go through the drive-through to get a salad for a quick lunch. You drive away and find a nice spot in the shade to park. You get your salad out, only to discover there is no fork, knife, or spoon included in the bag. You are hungry and frustrated, "I knew that guy at the window didn't have it together!"

Another time, you can't find your prescription sunglasses just as you are headed out the door. The thought would likely by something like, "I paid $350 for those glasses!" Inconvenience. Not what you thought your day would be like.

When our friend doesn't show, we get frustrated. We may start to think we must not be that important to them if they can't show up on time. We may even begin planning our exit strategy from the friendship. This is based on our thoughts about what people who are friends should act like—our ideas about friendship. Our friendship code is that a friend who blows off lunch is not a good friend.

When we realize we don't have utensils to eat our salad with, we try to think of where we might find at least a fork. We might empty out the complete contents of our glove compartment, look under the seats, think of where we could go pick up another fork, and yes—contemplate eating the salad with our hands. We were expecting that utensils would be in the bag.

When we can't find our sunglasses, we begin walking around and around to all the places we have been. We think hard. "Where did I last have them?" We spend a lot of time looking for them because we know they are lost.

Each interruption to a good day frustrates us. We grumble and scold ourselves and others for failings. Self-doubt. Annoyance at why this happens to us.

Whether you feel like you need a better quality of friend, need to check the bag before driving off from the drive-through, or need to be more careful about where you put your sunglasses—you are doing it right! You are responding to the information you know at the time.

It's the same for our life. Disappointments in life can easily make us think our life is not good—broken.

That's why I am so cheerful. Maybe a party is the farthest thing from your mind when your relationship is broken or you think your sex life sucks or you don't have one. Maybe the thought of sexual problems when sex "is pretty good right now, thank you" makes you want to close this book right now.

I get that my optimism seems plain wrong.

It may not feel like it, but you are doing it right! You are responding to what you know. The key is to find out what you don't know you don't know. Look for the new information. Question the story you have about sex. Don't fire your friend, go hungry, buy a new pair of sunglasses, or give up on sex. Wake up and pay attention to your story.

What If?

What if we discover that the lunch date was really an hour later—when we recheck our calendar, it says so. Aha! We were going by what we thought. We didn't know what we didn't know. Our mind had a story about friendship. We just followed the River of our Mind.

What if the utensils to eat the salad are in a premade pocket in the salad bowl? We will not go without lunch after all! Aha. We were swept along by the story that the utensils are always in the bag.

What if our sunglasses are flipped up on our heads? So embarrassing and what a waste of fifteen minutes looking for them. Aha! We just rolled with the story that they were lost. We missed that one.

It's easy to let the River of our thoughts sweep us along.

What if there is stuff we don't know, a different story about sex? In the same way that we can discover new information on a daily basis, sex not going well can be an opportunity to find a new story.

When sex starts going wrong, people tend to feel lousy about it because it doesn't match up to their personal story of sex. Yet they just float with it.

It's a normal part of life to be upset with a friend who is late, that we will have to skip lunch, that we have lost the sunglasses.

It's normal to think and want sex to be good, and to be disappointed when it's not.

What a relief to find out that we didn't know what we thought we knew about our relationship and sex.

Woohoo, we get to have lunch with our friend and laugh at our mistake. What a relief that we can eat our salad. What a relief that our sunglasses are found—we are humbled!

Woohoo, you are doing it right! Your unhappiness is a chance to get to more accurate information—your wisdom.

You don't know what you don't know. You are normal.

I think you are going to be ready to party when you discover that "you are doing it right!" When you realize that the way to feel good about your relationship and your sex life is to find out what you don't know that you don't know—yet! It is an unknown, untraveled place in your life.

The really good part!

Campfire

A Place to Tell Your Story

Coming to therapy is hard for most people.

Let's just take this a step at a time.

First thing, find my office and park in the back. Follow the sign to my office door. Put the door code in. 6300. Please take a seat in the waiting area. In a few minutes, I will come down the stairs to greet you. I will lead the way up the stairs and into my office.

Here's where you sit.

Tell me your story. It may be helpful to think of my office like a campfire at night. It's a place where people tell stories. A place to hear a story, and maybe understand something new.

To help you tell your story, I am likely to ask questions. Questions like:

- How do you feel about this relationship? (Or the fact that you don't have a relationship?)
- What makes you happiest in this relationship?
- What is most disappointing about this relationship?
- What does intimacy mean to you?
- When have you been the happiest?
- How close are you with other people?
- When was a time when sex was good for you?
- What would a good sex life look like?
- Are you able to climax?

It doesn't seem like a place to tell your story at first. There is no beautiful fire dancing in the dark to catch your eye and draw you to sit for a while. No, quite the opposite. It does not seem like an inviting campfire. It takes courage to show up for therapy.

When you sit in the fading yellow oversized leather chairs in my office, you know you will be talking about uncomfortable things. You imagine it will be about what you do wrong, or what you should do, or sex. And with a person you don't know! Most of us would dread that.

Hope nudges a person's courage. The hope that I can help them feel better, or get through to their partner.

I know that many worry, "What will she ask me to do? Will this be all my fault? Will my partner get off the hook again? Will I be embarrassed and humiliated when I can't do this technique, or don't want to explore the erotic stuff?"

Quite a few who come to work on their sex life wonder if they will have the courage to say that thing they have long wanted to say to their partner. Most just want to quit worrying about sex. There can be a lot to overcome before sitting down in my office.

Clients come anyway. They come because they are miserable. They come as a last-ditch effort to make their sex "fails" go away. They come because their partner says they must. They come to fix their partner. They come because they love each other.

They come and tell their story of their unhappiness with their relationships and sex:

- I am unhappy in this relationship.
- I'm never going to find a partner.
- I have lost my libido.
- My partner and I don't have chemistry.
- My needs are not being met.
- I don't have a partner and dating sucks.
- Sex just isn't that important to me.
- I am broken.
- Sex is very important to me.
- My partner doesn't love me.
- I made a mistake.
- I love my partner, but I am not in love.

Each is an important story, but it isn't the story that is most important. Each story is about Self and how a person understands their Self.

It's good to talk about your relationship and sex. To tell your stories out loud. To be aware of what you are telling yourself and where you are getting information about yourself.

I will listen and honor your stories. And then I will ask you "What if?"

The Real Story
Let's Find Yours

Here's the thing. A person's story of their relationships, sex, and unhappiness isn't the real story. At least it's not the story I'm looking to see.

Like a detective, I take a record of the story. I make notes on my ever-present pad of paper. I piece together details that will make for a big reveal. Only my job isn't to find who done it, who is to blame. My job is to find what's missing in the story. There is always something missing. The stories reveal what is missing.

And I already know what's missing for most people.

My work is to help a person understand what's missing. They need to know what's missing if they are going to do the work to find it. My most important job is helping my clients locate the missing piece. I can't do it for them. In fact, no one—not even their partner or future partner—can do it for them.

I listen intently to each story. I am on the lookout for the part in the story that tells what shape their Self is in—a status report of their Self. Our stories always paint a picture that tells whether we are an awake Person Self in our Boat Bodies on our River Minds.

As a person tells me about their relationship, dating experiences (or lack of dates), sex life, or lack of sex life, what fingerprint-like evidence begins to lead me to the most important question about their Self? Is the Person's Self awake?

Yet I can't just come out and pronounce, "Aha! you are sleeping!" I have to find a way to help the person actually wake up. Wake up in real time about their story and be able to ask the "What if?"

It is usually helpful to use the working verdict a person has about their self or their partner.

Something is wrong with me. I am not desirable. I am broken. I'm fat. I'm not really a sexual person. I think I'm with the wrong partner. I am not a real man. Why do men need sex so much?

Even when a person tells me about their partner, the words they use reveal how they understand their Self. What is the working verdict a person has about their partner?

My partner has let themselves go. I think my partner was abused. I don't turn my partner on. My partner isn't into my kind of sex play or lifestyle. My partner is into weird sex. My partner is Asexual. My partner is sex negative. There are not any good partners out there!

So, for example, when we are unhappy (anxious, worried, ashamed, disappointed, frustrated, angry) with our sex life, it's often because of what our sex stories are telling us about our Self.[2]

Our sense of our Sexuality comes from the stories we have about sex and what those stories tell us about our Self. Many stories cause us to pass over our What Is. Just one story can lull our Self to sleep. A sleeping Self is a missing Self.

I want to understand what a person is telling themselves based on their unique experience of sex. As they tell me about scenes from their sex life, what do they say about themselves? What do they feel good about? What do they criticize themselves for?

What do they put on their partner? My partner does not turn me on. My partner does not "get" sex. I think my partner was abused.

Most people who come for help have ideas of what needs to happen. They have accepted their self-imposed verdict and are hoping that changing their relationship, getting their partner to change, changing the way they have sex, the kind of sex, how often they have sex, changing their libido, or changing to another partner can reverse the judgment.

"Is there any hope for me?"

"Is there any hope for us?"

I know there is more than hope. There is the option of a complete overturn of the verdict.

First, let's find the story you tell yourself about relationships and/or about sex. Let's start with your story.

---

2   Our stories often help us navigate around and ease our discomfort, pain, or trauma. When a story causes pain or discomfort we tend to question or blame ourselves rather than question the story. This is because we view our Self based on the story. The truth of our Inner Person Self is the wisdom we can seek to untangle us from the story.

Aha!
A Wake-Up Moment

My first session with Marc and Kiersten went well. They are back for their second session and share that they feel relieved to have unburdened themselves and to have someone who knows how to help, who has a plan. They left last session with a sense that they could get over this. They had a very good week and have even taken a whirl with sex already!

This is good to hear. Quite a few couples come back to that second session and report they feel worse after their first session. More on that later, but for now coming back in a happy mood shows that the couple has some day-to-day positives, communication, and respect for each other. They have some Intimacy skills and can be Intimate.[3] I think they are ready for their first Aha moment.

That moment you see something in a new, unexpected light is what I call an "Aha moment." It's the moment you wake up and understand something new about yourself or your world.

My own journey into what I didn't know I didn't know came at my very first sex therapy seminar.

I had recently graduated with my Master in Community Counseling degree. I was working on my required hours under supervision to get my state license.

I had decided at the last minute to attend a counselor training to finish off continuing education requirements. The presenter was Dr. David Schnarch; his book *Passionate Marriage* had just come out. I was expecting to hear more about sex—to get more informed about different kinds of sex, how to be more sexy, more aroused, how to understand what made people more compatible as sex partners, and how to help my clients with sexual dysfunction.

---

3   I do not use the word "intimacy" as a euphemism for sex. I define "Intimacy" as the ability to experience another person while at the same time staying with and holding onto your own experience.

Until I heard Dr. Schnarch speak, I did not know what I did not know. My Aha was that it was very exciting to focus on the interaction between partners before, during, and after sex. If sex wasn't going well, the answer was not so much to work on sex, but to work on the interaction, the Intimacy between the partners. I got a new refreshing picture of Intimacy.

Sex and Intimacy are not the same. Aha!

Though we often blend them together, they are not the same. I had gone to the seminar to get training to help my clients with sex. I came out inspired to learn as much as I could about how two people experience each other. Intimacy. Before that weekend, I had not given much thought to intimacy. In fact, it just seemed like a polite way to say sex.

It's great to start a second session in good standing; it doesn't always happen and it may not last. For all my talk about throwing a party, the party doesn't just throw itself. That's okay. Regardless of whether I have happy campers or not, we have work to do.

Marc and Kiersten are here because Marc is having trouble with his erections. The problem has worsened as both their feelings of anxiety about sex have increased. So much so that they have started to avoid touching and are avoiding sex altogether.

In our first session, we began preparing for exploration of Sexuality by discussing the words and their meanings. Today, after that first trip into unknown ground, this couple follows me more easily. I want to hear more of their story of sex and what that story is telling this couple.

I begin by asking "What did you learn about your sex story at our last session?"

Kiersten starts, "I did not realize how much each of us have been struggling."

Marc quickly adds, "I hadn't realized how much dread and anxiety I have built up. I didn't realize Kiersten was so worried about how to approach me. I just thought she was hurt that I wasn't attracted to her."

They had both been surprised as they began to talk to each other about how hard it had been to deal with the self-doubt and anxiety both of them were feeling.

They had been trying to work through their sex problem with stories about themselves that had the "yes or no, either or" thinking.

We talk about what they have done to try to fix this problem. Kiersten answers that she has tried to set up more date nights, wear more lingerie to bed, and be enthusiastic in affectionate words and gestures. When they do have sex, she works to pace with him to try to keep the energy up.

Marc says he has gotten Cialis, looked at porn, masturbates "to check the equipment," and tries to fantasize during the day and during sex to get more tuned into feeling sexual.

I listen carefully. They are telling me what they know about sex and what they want out of sex. Marc "knows" his libido and erections are broken. Kiersten "knows" she isn't getting Marc excited enough to have an erection. This is their sex story.

It is clear that their "goals" (to meet sex needs) are creating the problem. The story goes that Marc "needs" to perform, to get a reliable erection, to satisfy his partner and himself. Kiersten "needs" to feel spontaneity that would reassure her of Marc's desire.

It's as if Marc and Kiersten are boats without paddles or a rudder. They are swept up in the current and being flung wherever the river takes them.

It is highly unlikely with Cialis or no Cialis that this couple's sex life will get better without some change. In fact, as they have shared, their goals for their sex life have only increased their discomfort. Luckily, we can go to a place they don't know they don't know to turn this problem around.

It starts with looking at the story of sex. The need for performance, or the need for spontaneity. If you need performance, you will focus on performing—getting that penis erect and keeping it hard.

If you need spontaneity, you will focus on how sex starts. Arousal needs to seem spontaneous, not like it is a chore your partner is only doing to please you. The manner in which sex starts reassures you that your partner really does want to have sex—that your partner desires you.

Marc and Kiersten's story of sex is wreaking havoc on them.

I say, "You will recall that we have said your goal in sex will determine how you invite your partner for sex and what you do to have sex. This means we can change the goal and we will get a different result. Luckily, our Sexuality points the way. When sex is going well, we feel good about ourselves, and good that our partner desires sex with us. We feel desirable. When sex isn't going well, it's time, it's our signal to go to a different place. We are being called to a different experience of sex."

They have been trying to make sex better by working on getting more aroused. This is a normal response to what you know. Marc doesn't initiate sex if he doesn't feel like he can get and keep an erection. Kiersten tries to be sure to look sexy and act sexy. They are stuck trying to get their needs met and very stuck on erections.

This couple is working to make the problem better by working directly on their sexual performance. To be blunt, they are trying to get that erection working. It is understandable. And it is normal to respond to the information that you have.

We turn onto the path of Sexuality. What does it mean that Marc is having difficulty with his erections? Does it mean that Marc has a sexual dysfunction?

I invite them to come with me down a path they have never walked before.

"What if not getting an erection meant something different than a dysfunction?"

I pause.

"What if Marc's erection difficulty is actually a good sign?"

Both Marc and Kiersten rivet their wide eyes to mine. "What?" They are both unsure.

I continue. "I think that losing an erection can be an important signal. Remember, when sex isn't going well, I'm all about throwing a party and celebrating. That's because this is an important signal that will help you. The key is reading the signal correctly."

"What if we discover that the erection is really helping to communicate something important to Marc? What if this problem with erection was like the time our friend didn't show for lunch or we didn't get a fork to eat our salad and we were responding to the wrong information? What if we are reading the meaning of the signal wrong?

I ask them to think about their response thus far in trying to get past the "erection problem."

Marc shares how he feels like he hasn't had any success at all in getting reliable erections. In fact, it seems more and more impossible. He feels defeated.

"My erection problem has gotten to the point that I think about it a lot throughout the day. I carry a constant dread about it. It's gotten to where Kiersten reaches out to hug me and I instantly tense up because I think, 'What if she wants to have sex?'"

Marc continues, "Lately, every time I do feel aroused and I initiate. It starts out fine, but I think we both rush things in hopes that my erection will stay. I haven't been able to keep my erection for longer than a few minutes. When I lose it, all I can think about is, I have let Kiersten down. I get so ashamed that I have to get up and leave the room."

I offer a summary: "So, the more you try to fix the problem, the bigger and more discouraging the problem becomes. In your discouragement you are not able to talk or support each other. You are becoming more distant from each other."

I see them both nod.

I repeat the question, "What if you not having an erection meant you weren't ready for sex? What if instead of saying it's not working, you thought, 'There's the signal'? What if the meaning of no erection wasn't that you're not excited enough, but that you weren't ready?

"Marc, I think your loss of erection is a signal, not a failure. It is a signal that something is missing."

Aha! I see both Marc and Kiersten relax back into their chairs. They are ready to find out what they don't know they don't know. To find what is missing.

Lost in the Story

Our Stories Sedate Our Inner Person Self

Your Sexuality is like a book of all the stories you have about sex and what those stories tell you about your Self.

It's very easy to get lost, be hopelessly adrift in a story of sex. This holds the same with good stories and miserable stories.

Marc and Kiersten's story of their sex life is that they are dysfunctional and broken. Kiersten's story is that she isn't desirable enough to get Marc aroused. Marc's story is that his body is malfunctioning.

It's as if their Boat Bodies are adrift on their River Minds, the stories in the River swirling all around. Meanwhile, Marc's Self and Kiersten's Self are each asleep, not awake. Their Inner Person Selves are missing.

What if Marc not having an erection is not a malfunction, but rather a correct response to the way this couple is trying to have sex? They come to sex with their stories of sex, hoping that the Boat will cooperate, that the River will take them where they want to go. They are so focused on their story of sex that neither one of them is showing up for sex.

They may both get naked, but neither Self is awake and present. Marc's body is communicating to him. I think it goes something like, "Hey, buddy, slow down. There's something missing here." What if there was a better way to have sex? What if you didn't need to will yourself to have an erection and to be so worried about hurting Kiersten's feelings? Marc's Body is saying no to his story of sex. Marc's Body is inviting him to wake up.

How the Body Asks "What If?"

What Is the Body Saying to Us?

In fact, the Body is the part of a human that is the best at asking "What if?"

Our Bodies do not speak to us in words, but in a language of sensation and energy. Our Bodies store information—they have an excellent memory and can instantly get messages and memories to our Minds in the form of thoughts and images.

Our Bodies can communicate with us through images, mental movies, sensations, or sounds from our history. Our Bodies give us pain signals. Without any thought that we need to think, our Body will fight, flee (flight), or freeze, in order to protect us. We can feel sexual arousal instantly ignite our Bodies. Our Bodies can usher us into a flow state that feels like we are outside of our Minds and thoughts and observing ourselves. We can transcend both our thoughts and Bodies for a time of awareness and clarity that only comes when we are fully awake, fully alive in the present. This is the runner's high of an athlete, the creative flow of an artist, the Erotic Flow of a sexual experience, the awe and elation of experiencing something unimaginably vast, wondrous, and beyond ourselves like art or nature.

Pain, fight or flight, sexual energy, flow states, and experiences of awe: these are all Body things. Our Boat Bodies are skillful at getting us important information. And getting it to us immediately.

For example, before we think, "Oh, that car is suddenly stopping!" our Body has already calculated the "What if?" and moved to help us. When driving we see brake lights on the car ahead and we instantly hit the brake because our Bodies have already asked "What if we rear-end that car?"

This is our Fight or Flight response, and it's faster than our Mind.

Sexual arousal is another example of the Body asking "What if?"

Unlike the Fight or Flight response, most of us are very slow at figuring out what the Body is really telling us when we have sexual feelings, or are turned on.

I know, I know. Insert clever responses and jokes here. "Duh, when you get turned on, your body is saying it wants to have sex!" Yes, that is a funny one.

When we feel sexual arousal, it is because our Body is saying yes to the story that is presented.

If our Person Self is asleep in our Boat Body and we are just drifting along wherever our River Mind current pulls us, we take the ride in our Boat. It is often a thrilling ride and it fits the stories we have of ourselves perfectly. We are sexy. We are a good lover. We fulfill our Role. Check. We are sexual. We deserve pleasure. We perform. Check. Check. Check. Someone wants to have sex with us and we want to have sex with them. We are bona fide, validated, worthy. All stories that make us feel good.

Through the heightened sensation of our sexual response, each of our Bodies has the sensual and erotic language by which it communicates the "What if?" question very clearly.

Through our engaged senses and our sexual response wake-ups, the Body is communicating to our Mind that something is resonating, filling in a missing piece for a puzzle in our story of Self. The missing piece may have been missing for many years. Something about the arousal says, "What if you are worthy? What if you are desirable? What if you are lovable? What if you had power?" We are instantly awake and paying attention. Life is great. Life is good in this awakened state.

Sexual turn-ons show us our stories, and there are stories when we don't get turned on. If for some reason we are not sexually aroused in what is supposed to be a sexual experience, the Body is still showing us our story at the moment.

When we are still sleeping, still at a Latent, Performance, or Validation understanding of ourselves, we go with these stories. We don't look at or question the stories that turn up. And they usually are enough to provide us with a nice wake-up. An orgasm. Wonderful orgasm. It is the moment that a human can fully feel alive and whole and worthy of love. But an orgasm can be like a car without an alternator. When the orgasm ends, the Person Self slips right back into unconsciousness. Right back to drifting in the River of Thought.

What are these "stories" that turn us on? Every story that arouses us sexually is a story about how we want to feel about ourselves.

We have sex and it feels like we are a good lover. Or not. Our partner wants to have sex and we achieve a climax. Or not. We notice our partner wants to have sex with us or we want to have sex with them. Or not.

It is the "or not" that throws us off. Those are where the stories get interesting. The "or not" stories are when we can see the clues about the Self. It is an important event. When the story doesn't go according to what is supposed to be the story, it is a great time to ask "What if?"

How to Be Sexual
Check Your Goal for Sex

I get to my office a little early this morning to finish some paperwork. I open my schedule to check who I have scheduled for my counseling day. I see a new client, Shatima, for my first session. Shatima has a painful mystery. The mystery is her dating life. She has tried everything she could think of to fix herself.

I remember talking with her last week on the phone as we on-boarded her for sex therapy. Shatima is single—not on purpose. "I want help to learn how to be sexual", she told me. "So I can meet partner."

At 10 a.m. I go down the stairs to meet her. Shatima could be a model. She is gorgeous. She has a wide and easy smile with ever-so-perfect teeth. She is tall and slender with a jaunty twisted afro. Her skin is a sleek, glowing brown.

Shatima had been using online dating for a couple years before she made the journey up the stairs to my office to get help with a problem she is having with dating.

She begins.

"I'm thirty-one now. I have never had a long-term boyfriend. In college I would a date a guy for a few weeks, but then they would break it off or would ghost me. It didn't bother me that I hadn't found a partner because I have been focusing on my career and finishing my grad degree.

"Three years ago, I decided that I needed to focus on finding a partner. I want to have children and a family. So, I started on a couple of dating sites.

"I get lots of responses. I ignore many of them because they aren't my type or are too old or young. I'm pretty choosy and careful. I have met some good guys and some duds.

"My problem is that I go on a date with someone who seems very attractive to me, and after one or two dates when we have sex, I never hear from them again.

"I want your help because I don't think I know how to be sexual. Something is wrong with me. I'm embarrassed to say I don't have an orgasm. I don't think I ever have. I need you to teach me how to have sex."

She continues. "You know, I've been trying to keep myself attractive. I work out just about every day. I am very careful about my skin treatments, and I try to read up about what men like in bed."

She has come to a sex therapist to learn about sex. She feels like she is missing something. And she's worried that she's broken.

She is trying everything she knows to be sexy and to get sex right, but time after time the men she meets ghost her. She wants to work on the how-to, the performance of sex, so that she will be sexual.

She isn't broken. However, she is missing something. In her pursuit of a partner, she has left out the most important part: her Self.

"What if you have it backwards?" I ask. "You are trying to find sex in yourself. Am I sexual? You want to know how to be sexual.

"What if it's the other way around? What if you started with adding your Self in the sex? Check in with yourself? Ask, 'How does my Body feel in a sexual encounter? What if before you agree to have sex, you ask yourself if you want to have sex? How do I feel when I am talking to this person? Does this date listen to me? Do I feel good spending time with this person?'

"What if you checked in with your Thoughts and what your Body was feeling in the situation? What if you make a decision to have sex because you want to have sex. Not as a step for checking compatibility, or getting someone to love you.

"You can choose the best Match.com profile that ticks all the boxes. But the real match is to bring your Self to the date."

Shatima and I begin a back-and-forth discussion to help her locate her Self in these experiences.

Halfway through our session, I stand up to draw the arousal pathway graph on my whiteboard.[4] We discuss that the goal for most people who have sex is to have an orgasm. I point out that from what she has shared so far, she isn't even thinking about an orgasm for herself.

Her story of sex is that she needs to be sexy and sexual enough to satisfy a potential partner. This story of sex has caused her to feel broken and not sexual at all.

4　An illustration of Part 1 and Part 2 of the Arousal Pathway Graph is located in the upcoming Awakeness Section in the chapters "How to Do Sex" and "How to Show Up for Sex."

As I lay out the arousal pathway, we discuss that if you change the goal, you change the experience. If her goal is to have an experience with her partner, then she needs to be in the experience.

We continue our work together. I review anatomy and physiology and what we know about women's experiences of sex. She is surprised to find that she had been trying to have sex like her male partners. As we work to get her more knowledgeable about her Body, she excitedly says, "I didn't know that. That's what I have been missing!"

In her dating experiences, not only does she approach the experiences in a sex-focused way, but she also has only been showing up to the dates to try to be what she thought men needed her to be.

She is missing in the experiences.

I was inviting Shatima to wake up in her Boat. She has been sedated by her River Mind too long.

"Oh, so I was right! I don't know how to be sexual!" she says enthusiastically, and continues, "I am trying to be what my partners need me to be. I am responding to their sexuality. I am not awake to my own sexual responses."

We continue to discuss "What if?" What if she stayed present to herself and her experience when meeting someone for the first time? What if she didn't focus on her partner's desire to have sex and actually decided whether she would like to have sex? Her story up to this point was that if you want to be a good date, you have sex with them if they want to have sex.

We discuss being awake and present to her own sexual response instead of waiting to respond to a partner.

The "What ifs" keep coming. What if she didn't automatically have sex because someone else expected it? What if she paid attention to her own pleasure during sex? She had discovered that she was so focused on the other partner, she hadn't even thought about her own enjoyment.

By checking the stories Shatima had about sex and what that story told her about Self, we discovered that she, her Self, has been missing in her dating experiences.

She is waking up to the What Is of sex and how to show up for sex.

PART TWO

My "What If?" Journey

Not Content

I very much wanted to find what I was missing.

"It" had happened again. This time while hiking with a friend. I kept having conversations with friends—good friends—that left me feeling ashamed and completely exhausted. The reason was that before I realized it was happening, I would start to rant and could not stop myself. I would repeat and repeat until both my friend and I fell silent with fatigue.

When this happened, I realized I was not Content. I did not have peace. The rant had brought a storm that had me going through the same story over and over.

"What's wrong with me? Why can't you keep your mouth shut? You call yourself a counselor?"

It would take me a few days to revive and move on. I would journal and read to find thoughts and ideas to help. Sometimes, I could apologize to the friend. Other times, I would make another promise to myself that I wouldn't lose it like that again. I pictured it as throwing up emotions all over my friend. I knew it wasn't pleasant.

I couldn't understand why after working so hard to process my painful emotions in life, studying relationships for my work as a counselor, and successfully helping clients do their work, I would have these dysfunctional outbursts.

I decided I was missing something about myself. So, I decided to go back to counseling.

Painting
Boat. River. Person.

It is my first counseling session. The painting is the first thing I see as I walk into Lindy's office. You can't miss it. The painting is very tall and very wide and covers the entire side wall. A live tree in a ceramic pot sits gracefully at the edge of the painting. The tree leans in and casts soothing shade over the flowing green-blue river that carries a boat. There is a person in the boat.

The scene is beautiful. A person in a boat on a river. The bright, lush blues, purples, yellows, and greens invite attention.

With effort, I pull my focus back to Lindy as I sit down. I am determined to remember my clear purpose, the reason I made this appointment to see a counselor.

Whatever spell the painting is trying to put me under, I have a story that I need someone to hear. I am finally clear about how to say it and I am ready to tell it.

Lindy invites me to sit as she sits opposite me.

"Welcome," she says warmly. "Where would you like to begin?"

I say my nice "straight to the point" goal. This feels good. I am proud. I will not hurriedly try to tell her all the ins and outs of my life as if I am so desperate to have someone hear me. Although I am. I will not make her work to help keep me focused and clear about why I am here. I want to be a good client. And I want to show that I too am a competent and insightful therapist.

"I want help with my meltdowns."

There. I have begun to tell my story to a counselor. I hope Lindy is listening. I hope she can help me.

Counseling

Looking for What I didn't Know I didn't Know

When I decide to find a counselor, to work on my pain, I start journaling about the issue—a lot. I search my emotions to find my pain and to clearly state what I need help with. I write and write in my notebook to ease the dread and anxiety about working with a counselor again.

I have had this problem for a lot of years. I make many promises to myself about how not to rant out of control again, and sometimes I succeed. Even when I am able to keep it together ever so carefully, I feel like I am fake and am holding back. Whether I rant or not, I feel defeated. I don't want to ignore this pain anymore.

I can't figure it out. Why do I keep losing it in an otherwise nice conversation? I can't seem to find the real story here. Something is missing. I am ready for what I don't know I don't know.

I am very clear that my story always leaves me with a deep shame.

Meltdowns

Lindy's Answer

"What happens, what is the meltdown like for you?" Lindy asks.

I have prepared for this.

"I have these times when I suddenly feel like there is a buildup of ideas and sentences that are in my mind. It's like they all start pushing to get out at the same time. Like I need to say each one. I talk faster and louder to try to let each one free. It feels like I have a breach in the dam and there is nothing I can do about it."

As I hear myself say this, I imagine Lindy is immediately thinking "emotional flooding" and has the follow-up thought, "You call yourself a counselor?"

I continue on to say that these meltdowns usually happen when I am with trusted friends. Although it has happened several times in a group of friends, and once at a professional workshop. But mostly, it happens when I have a conversation with caring friends.

I notice she is intently listening. I tell her about my latest conversation with a friend as we hiked together.

"What were you and your friend talking about?"

I pause a beat. I feel a slight warmth rising in my face. I never thought to check the subject matter! I push embarrassment aside; I will be brave.

"I guess with that friend we usually end up talking about 'the church.' She and I grew up in the same church. Only I and my husband left that church quite some time ago. Since she's a friend I feel I can be deeply honest with, I have talked with her a lot about my experiences.

"I wish I wasn't so needy. I don't really have a lot of people to talk to. So when I do talk to people, it's like I lose control, I can't stop talking!" I add as an out-loud explanation that I have often said to myself.

Lindy asks, "Are there other topics where you have had these meltdowns?"

"My family." After a pause, I add, "My marriage." I feel nervous.

I quickly say, "I have done a lot of work on all three over the years. I worked with a counselor for a few years and reading helps me a lot."

I also add, "The work I do with my counseling clients really has taught me a lot. I have come so far. I'm much better than I used to be."

It feels like I need to let Lindy know that I have been working on myself. It's what good counselors do.

"So, what you are saying is that this is a trusted friend. She was willing to hear your story. It was safe to talk with her. As you talked with her, you opened your heart and there were words and emotions that rushed out like a flash flood. It's like there is too much water for the dam that is holding it back."

Hmm. I don't like what she is saying. I feel broken. A part of me wants to protest, "I've done my work!" I look at her trying to see what her take is. I am checking to see if I need to tell her, "I know what emotional flooding is, I just want to find out why!"

I choose silence.

I do a quick mental check-in with myself. The session feels okay. So far, it has gone according to my plan. It seems like Lindy is following my story. I have been able to talk calmly and not go off topic for my goal of getting rid of these rant meltdowns.

I take a deep breath to focus my attention. This feels like the important part. I will wait for it. The key to fixing this problem. The good part.

Lindy's next question interrupts me right off my planned path.

"Have you looked at this painting?" She points to the left.

"What? Huh? There's no way to miss it!" I say to myself silently as I turn and look at the wall with the gigantic painting.

"It's hard to miss!" I say out loud, trying to sound lighthearted. My mind is still waiting on the church, parents, and marriage thing.

"The painting will show you why you have meltdowns!" Lindy says with confident enthusiasm.

With that, the fifty-minute session is over.

After Session
Thinking

My first session with Lindy gives me lots to think about. I can't decide if Lindy has pointed out the painting as a tactful way to wrap up the session or if she was serious about the painting being part of the counseling work.

Overall, I have a feeling of optimism that she will have some wisdom to help me get rid of this problem I have.

At home, I think about the session and the painting. I pull out my journal, a college-ruled notebook, and begin writing again. I write my thoughts as they come to me and then go back to see what I have written. This usually helps me get clarity, to get my thoughts focused and process my emotions.

Okay, so the painting has a boat, an artsy, imperfectly painted boat. Outside-the-lines type of brush strokes in purple and pink came together to actually make what looks like a boat. Hmm. A purple and pink boat.

Shamrock green with improbable blotches of shiny blue surround the boat, yet somehow show the movement of a river. One particularly heavy blue square-ish area looks like it has covered up a mistake. It reminds me of the painted square shapes that cover graffiti on a bridge or side of a building. The blues in the river don't match. Is it a whirlpool or something submerged in the river?

I wish I had taken a picture with my phone.

I continue to think and look over the painting in my thoughts. A sloppily painted boat that is moving along on the mysterious river. And what about the person in the boat on the river?

The face has distinct eyes that are open and intently looking ahead at something in the river. It seems like it is a woman, because of the long golden hair. But the straight posture and the torso turned to the side give no hint of the shape of the person's front. I ponder. Male or female? Men could have long hair, yet women could have a flat-ish chest.

I pull my attention back to the question. What does a boat on a river with a person have to help me with my meltdowns?

I turn to a blank page in my journal and write "Boat. River. Person."

Second Session
The Painting Speaks

As I drive to my second session, I review my counseling situation again.

The reason I am in counseling is that I am missing something. I have been over and over the problem. I have tried the "What ifs" and checked the story I am telling myself. Try as I may, I cannot connect the "What ifs" to these meltdowns. I don't know how to go where I don't know to go.

I think I know the story I am telling myself. It is really annoying to me that I have these meltdowns. I think through the years of self-care, self-soothing, and the work to learn to take care of my relationship with myself. I feel a familiar embarrassed warmth in my face. My shame momentarily pulls me into a confused and jumbled stream of words.

"Alright!" I say out loud. In the car I talk to myself. "What's my intention here?" I go silent again, but now my thoughts are clear. My intention is to push through discomfort. I make some commitments to myself. I won't be jealous of Lindy's beautiful painting or office, or the smooth way she closes her session with a neatly packaged statement to keep me thinking. I will not get defensive about my counseling skills. But mainly, I will work hard to work through the pain and the shame of these meltdowns. I'm determined.

As I enter Lindy's office, I realize I still am not sure about the painting. I glance at it as I take a seat across from Lindy. I feel a slight heaviness in my breathing.

To my relief, Lindy asks how the weather was for my drive. I relax as we chit-chat back and forth about the seasons we like.

There is a brief pause, and Lindy is right back talking about the painting. I notice that same sureness in her eyes and voice.

"Let's look at this painting again. I love this painting! It has important wisdom."
We are both looking at the painting now.

"This painting has the answer to your meltdowns."

I think, "Well, at least she remembers the meltdown part."

Lindy turns to me. "Do you know where you are in the painting?"

I barely pause before I answer. This seems way too easy. "The person in the boat represents me. I am the person in the boat."

She quickly says, "Yes, you are!"

There is a pause. She looks at me for a moment, and then surprises me by saying, "Where else are you in the painting?"

"What?" I think loudly. "Where else am I in the painting?"

A flash thought of squares painted over graffiti pops into my head. The paint never quite matches and so you know what's under it. There is that part in the painting that seems like a weird cover-up. Is that me? I look at the painting. Is there some mirror reflection that I haven't seen yet?

Lindy interrupts the rabbit-hole my mind has started down to help me out.

"It's a trick question. The answer is that you are the Boat, you are the River, and you are the Person in the Boat on the River. The painting, the whole thing shows you—the complete you!"

I don't expect this. Well played, Lindy. I feel a resonance, some kind of recognition even though I still don't have a clue how this will help me with my work, my meltdowns. I am listening deeply.

Lindy continues, "Let's start with the Boat. It represents your Body. Your Body is the container, the physical part of you. The River is your Mind. The Boat is floating on the River and the River carries the Body." She looks at the painting, her eyes stopping at each part of the painting.

I am tracking so far. Boat Body. River Mind. Boat Body is influenced by the Mind, like a boat taken along by a river. I do know that what you think causes your emotions, and emotions are felt in the Body. It's making sense.

"The wisdom of this painting is that the Person sitting in the Boat is awake and watching the River, is paying attention to the Boat, and is paddling, directing the Boat to take them where they decide they need to go. The Person in the Boat is the "Awake Self." The Person Self is the captain, the one steering the Boat through the River. The captain watches the River Mind and pays attention and guides the Boat Body in order to take a journey.

"If the person is asleep, they and their Boat are taken wherever their River takes them.

"Each person has a Mind, Body, and an Inner Person Self. The Inner Person Self part is the most precious part of a human and yet it is the hardest to be aware of and keep awake. It's easy to focus on and immerse ourselves in the River. After all, the River of thoughts and images flows day and night. We are taken in by our thoughts. We respond and react to our thoughts without question. It's as if we are asleep in the Boat on the River. When we are not awake in our Boat on our River, we are at the mercy of where the River Mind takes our Boat Body.

"The River tells us stories about our Self. We accept and live the stories, without realizing they are only stories. It isn't truly what is. What Is is when the Self Person is awake in the Boat, and is guiding the Boat Body through the River Mind right there in the moment.

She gives an example. "Take football, either the American kind or the soccer kind—either one will do," she says lightheartedly. "Being awake in the Boat is actually playing a game, being a player. Most of us have parts in our lives where we are watching the game or match on TV, or at the very most go to a game and cheer from the stadium seats.

"When we are asleep in the Boat, we are watching the game, not playing the game. We are watching our River and taking in the story our Minds happen to be telling us about our Selves. You have to be in the game in the moment to know how to play the game. The 'What Is' happens when you are in the game on the field."

We spend time discussing the difference between being awake in the Boat, and sleepy or unconscious.

Then Lindy says, "Our time today is up. I have some homework for you. Next time I want you to tell me what a painting of your meltdowns would look like. Better yet, make a painting of your meltdowns!"

Assignment

Paint Your Meltdowns

Lindy has invited me to make a picture of my meltdowns. I immediately want to do it. It feels good. I can do artsy and creative. It's fun.

On the way home from session, I excitedly run through thoughts of my inventory of paints, watercolor pencils, and archival markers. Definitely watercolors! That's it. And where did I stash that watercolor sketchbook? I float happily on my River thoughts of future fun. I get to make a painting!

Counseling is fun!

Lindy is the best!

Thoughts

My River Mind

The next day my mood has changed.

As I wake up in bed, I feel unsettled. Like a lot of people, my morning thoughts sometimes bring me the solution to a problem I'm having, or a shift of mood. My mood does not feel good. My thoughts about making a picture about my meltdowns have taken a U-turn. I notice a slight sense of dread. I get out of bed to push away thoughts about painting.

Throughout the day the assignment keeps coming back up in my River Mind and I have extended conversations with myself.

I think about Lindy. What are her motivations? How will this help with getting rid of meltdowns?

I get the whole Mind, Body, Person thing. I know how to be awake and, in fact, I think I am more awake than a lot of people. For goodness' sake, I had been working with people to show up and open up in their relationships and sexuality for many years now. "3D" Sex. Emotional, mental, and physical intimacy. Sleepy Latent, Performance, or Validation Self. Awake Responsive Self. Integrated Self.

Counseling is stressful. I wonder if Lindy is forgetting I am a counselor. I'm not sure she realizes that I am a Sexuality and Intimacy specialist. Should I tell her? This assignment seems so basic.

On and on I float on my River thoughts.

I don't disagree that my meltdowns are because I am falling asleep to my Self. I just don't know why I am falling asleep when I work to be so purposeful in waking up in my life. I have worked and worked in my journals, with my friends, and in counseling to process my unfinished business about church, family, and my marriage. I am disappointed that I still fall asleep with such regularity.

I revisit my defense of me. I *have* worked on responding to people with who I know I am, not in defense of who I think they think I am.

I *have* studied and committed to practice kindness.

I work to be present and conscious in my life.

The more I think about the assignment, I feel my shame grow. An unending stream of stories about myself and the situation swirl and swirl in my mind. I do not stop to ask "What if?" in order to go to the place I didn't know I didn't know. I do not check my "What is?"—my real experience. I am not awake. I am not present.

Not yet.

I have so many conversations with myself and my stories of myself that I forget about painting a picture of my meltdowns.

I am asleep in my Boat and adrift on my River.

Wisdom of the Painting
Awakening Inner Person Self

Lindy was right. The Person in the Boat on a River painting did help me understand why I would "lose it."

I discovered that not being able to stop talking was actually the result of a wake-up moment, not a personal failing. It was like suddenly hitting your thumb with a hammer. My rant was like the wail of pain, or the profanity that bursts out as the pain hits.

After a couple of sessions with Lindy, an online article had helped me to ask the "What if I am angry?" question.

As I woke up to the What Is, I realized that I had not grieved the loss of a story of myself. Stepping away from being a certain kind of Christian brought the loss of my story. Being a Christian was a huge part of my external understanding of myself. When I asked the "What if?" I was able to step away from my church and wake up to my What Is.

At the same time, it brought the loss of validation from friends and family. Some responses were very painful. I was angry that my awakening knowing was minimized, and I was very sad that I was either left behind or needed to leave some relationships. I wanted to wake up. I wanted to find my true What Is. My meltdowns and the pain they caused me and my friends were what propelled me to locate my Self in the situation and begin to be awake and Responsive to my Inner Person Self.

In other words, I located and understood how to be a whole person. As long as I was asleep about the pain, I was at the mercy of my River. I was adrift in life and any conversation that touched near painful places.

I will always remember Lindy's words. "All of it—the whole painting is you!"

A Person Self in a Boat Body carried by a River Mind.

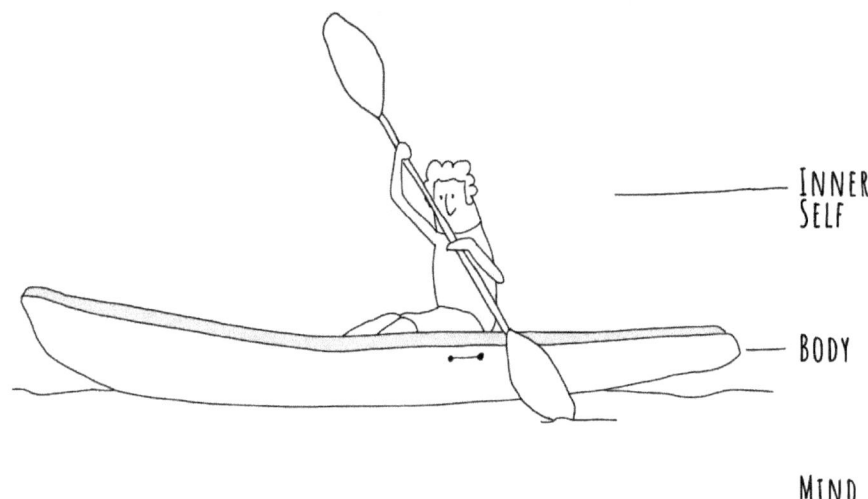

INNER
SELF

BODY

MIND

My Body Asks What If

Boat

Lindy had surprised me by pointing out that the painting in her office was a metaphor for a complete human. A whole person has a Boat Body, River Mind, and Inner Person Self.

Our Body is our vessel—the container of us.

Learning to understand our Body and receive information from our Bodies is easier if we are awake. Just as our Inner Person Self can think about thinking by watching the thoughts of our River Minds go by, our Inner Person Self can inspect our Boat Body and watch for warning signs and signals.

Going about our day to day, it's easy to slip into the idea that the thoughts in our mind are "me." It's easy to float on the current wherever the River takes us. To be lulled to sleep and not awake.

With Lindy's help, I discovered that my slipping into a rant was because I had entered back into the emotions of the situation that were painful and traumatic. My body was "speaking" with an energy that I was releasing in words. My rants were like I was a hockey play-by-play announcer (who wasn't very good at it) and the game wasn't going well.

I realized it was painful because I felt ignored and dismissed. It was traumatic because in these situations I emotionally stepped back into a sense of aloneness, rejection, and abandonment.

Up to the point of deciding to leave my family church, I had understood myself as belonging and meeting Christian expectations. I was accustomed to the abundant validation that we were "God's people." It is now much easier to see that my understanding of myself was dependent on people and situations outside of me.

Lindy had helped me understand how to think about my thinking and to pay attention to my Body's message. What if these rants were signals? What if these rants didn't mean I was broken in my emotional life and a self-focused person who used their friends to vent? What if my Body Boat was trying to tell me something?

My Body was signaling me that I had feelings of being unheard, alone, and isolated. I had been passing over these emotions as if I didn't have them, as if they were unimportant. I was not awake; I was adrift. Although I am still working on waking up and paddling through my Mind in my Inner world, I still am particularly aware when people change the subject, go silent—respond with silence, pick up their phone, or look at their smart watch in the midst of a conversation.

Our Bodies can do that. The Body is very smart.

From Outside to Inside
Waking Up

Waking up. It means that you start to examine your stories of self and begin to be alert and present to your Self. What is this Self? One way to think of it is to imagine there is a "seat" that is above the River of your Mind. Maybe you can think of the tall chair of a tennis umpire by the court or lifeguard by the water's edge—something raised up to get a better look. Picture going to sit in that up-high seat and watch the River go by and scan your Boat for messages. The part of you that can watch the River, scan your Boat, and notice everything in your immediate outside surroundings is your Inner Person Self. Waking up means that you are there on your seat, awake, conscious, present. You are not thinking to the future or dwelling on the past. You are awake to What Is now.

When we wake up, we move from looking at our Self from an outside perspective, and go inside. We take a seat inside. We sit down in the What Is; we are awake and present.

That was Marc and Kiersten's work. I wanted them to be present, to wake up their Inner Person Self during their sexual activities. I began to teach them to approach their sexual activities by searching for the What Is. To be sexual together from the inside. To have sex while awake.

That was Shatima's work. Going from Outside to Inside.

That was my work. To find the What Is of my true experience, not just the story I was telling myself to feel better.

WHAT IS

What Is?

The most important question you will ever ask is "What is?" Ask it often.

This is the journey. The journey to being awake and present in your life.

You start by paying attention to your "Aha's" and wake-up moments, and being willing to practice asking "What if?"

When we ask "What if we are missing something?" we become ready to find what we don't know we don't know. When we ask "What if my story isn't the real story?" we are free to see, understand, and move into the What Is of the present.

When we have started to ask "What if?" we become ready to see What Is.

"What is?" in this moment, right now. "What is?" It is a very powerful question that gives us much wisdom. When we come to our What Is, we are Responsive and awake.

What Is is the most important thing you can know.

The next twelve chapters explore What Is and how looking for your truth and understanding and waking up your Inner Person Self changes your life.

Chapter: What Is Your Experience? You are the only one that can get to your truth, your What Is.

Chapter: Your Super Power Your ability to pay attention is your Super Power. You can use this Super Power to disentangle from your thoughts. You can choose where to direct your attention.

Chapter: Your Real You Use the Inner Self Check-in to find your wisdom.

Chapter: Equal Say So The I Count–You Count framework provides the principles for advocating for your truth, your What Is.

Chapter: The Good Fail You can use distress and discomfort to get to (and experience) What Is.

Chapter: Uncomfortable What ifs You can use distress with a partner to ask "What if?" and get to What Is.

Chapter: Naked Holding Practicing simple What Is with a partner.

Chapter: Code Zombie Sexual experiences can be a major sedative keeping our Inner Person Self deeply asleep.

Chapter: Email The idea of needing sex keeps us stuck paying attention to our Outside Self. As a result we don't trust our experience or our own desirability, lovability, okayness, or wisdom.

Chapter: Chess When we don't attend to, trust, or tolerate what's happening inside of us, we deliberately seek more Outside stories and sedation.

Chapter: Couples and the Canary The stories we have about ourselves, that we repeat to ourselves, may seem real to us, so much so that others believe them as well.

Chapter: Jamila Asks What Is We may not want to look at our inner experience because it is really painful.

What Is Your Experience?

No One Else Knows It

Lindy introduced me to her painting of a boat on a river with a person in the boat. This painting metaphor represents a couple of important ideas that will help you become more responsive to Self, which will make you more awake and wise.

First, the idea that the whole painting represents the parts of a whole person. Most of us are asleep most of the time. Our default mode is to take action, respond, and follow wherever the River thoughts of our Mind take us in our Body Boat. Unlike in Lindy's painting, our eyes are not open; we don't have our paddles ready to navigate through our thoughts to get to the wisdom we have there.

Secondly, the truth of our experience is often way off from where our River Minds are taking us. This then becomes our most important task. To look at our actual experience, not the story of our experience. No one else can do this for us. Our experience, the being awake in our Boat on our River, is always ours and ours alone.

We can find it, instead of sleepily ignoring it, by practicing the What Is. The What Is is both a question and a statement. In your search for your truth, you ask "What is?" When you have landed on your truth, you will be able to rest in your What Is.

Your experience, your truth cannot be argued with. At least, you will get better at not arguing with it when you honor your own knowing, your own Awakeness.

Often rather than a What Is check-in with what is happening with our Inner Person Self, we pay attention to Latent, Performance, and Validation thoughts and stories of our River Mind. The water thoughts of our Minds come from outside of us and there is a lot of it. It's pretty normal to just float wherever the currents of life take you, but it means you are asleep in your painting.

Your Super Power

Your Attention

*I once fell asleep in my counseling chair. Well, I almost fell
asleep. I guess it was close enough to be one of those stories.*

I had heard stories of therapists falling asleep. How, during a counseling session
and usually while the client was talking, their therapist fell asleep. For many
years, I felt like I would never be "one of those therapists."

My client was talking and I remember my eyelids kept insisting on closing.
I was fighting to keep them awake and to unobtrusively swallow my yawn. I was
startled to hear my client say, "Dr. Lisa, are you falling asleep on me?" Though
I try not to interrupt my sessions for any reason, this time I apologized and got
up to get a drink of water. I returned to the session embarrassed, but very much
able to pay attention again.

It might seem that a person would never be drifting off to sleep while talking
about sex. You also may be surprised to hear that when you work with a sex
therapist, you are not paying them to talk about sex, you are paying for their
skill and ability to pay attention. Yes, I do listen and talk about all things sex and
sexual. Yet I think that my ability to pay attention is my most valuable skill to
help my clients.

Paying attention is how you practice the What Is.

I pay attention to the story behind the story. The path that a client doesn't
know they don't know—that one.

In order to focus your attention, you must wake up. The good news is you
can wake up in any moment at any time. The challenge is the staying awake part.
Practicing What Is is how you meet that challenge. It's how you wake up.

Your ability to wake up, to ask "What is?" is your Super Power. And it is how
you find the real experience of you, your truth, your What Is.

Your Real You
Wise Self

I am not afraid of storms for I am learning how to sail my ship. – Louisa May Alcott, *Little Women*, 1868

Your truth. How do you find it and how do you know if it is the real truth?

The short answer is it is your reality. No one else experiences life in the exact way you experience it.

Your reality is not the story your River Mind tells you it is. Your reality is what you actually experience in the present moment. The present moment is a page in your book of your life. What is in this moment for you? What is happening for you both outside and inside right this moment? What is your subjective experience? You get to your real experience by turning your attention to your River Mind and Boat Body. You notice where your River Mind is taking you, and you check what your Boat Body is communicating with you right now in this moment. This is your real story, your experience—your truth.

Some time ago I heard someone say, "The definition of mental health is to understand and be in reality." One definition I've used for many years is "Reality is the state of things as they are, rather than as they may appear or might be imagined."

So, if your truth is based on your reality, how do you practice paying attention to your reality to find your truth? I would like to guide you to some ideas to get you started on tuning in to your truth.

The Inner Self Check[5]

The Inner Self Check is a list that you follow to focus your attention. When I put it on my whiteboard, I include:

- Thoughts

5 For a full illustration of the Inner Self Check-in that is a part of the I Count–You Count Dialog Chart, please see the chapter Code Zombie.

- Emotions, feelings, descriptions of how I feel
- Needs
- Wants, desires
- My behaviors, my "stuff" (e.g., areas that need improvement, actions I regret, personal challenges)
- Body sensations
- Body energy levels
- Body messages

You can do this anywhere, anytime. I suggest you write it down. Handwriting accesses both sides of our brain, the emotional response side (right side of brain) and the logic and language side, the place where we make decisions (left side of brain). By handwriting, you gain information from your Body, not just your Mind. In the future, perhaps we will find out that when babies interact with a computer before they write it allows this same full-brain response, but for now I like the idea of not being on an electronic device to enter into a quiet space. A space that allows us to turn our full attention to our Inner space and Self.

It is helpful to track your Inner space daily if you are in a stressful period of your life, and to do it when you need clarity with a crisis event that heightens the thoughts and emotions in your Mind. It is a way of asking "What is my truth?"

When you have some clear answers to "What is my truth?" the answers allow you to paddle your Boat wherever you want to go on your River. Take your truth very seriously. Protect it. Review it. You can recheck it as often as you need, but hold on to your truth—your What Is.

"What is?" starts as a question, and then the answer becomes a statement. "What Is."

When you get to What Is, hold onto it. If you lose sight of your What Is, then turn it back into a question, "What is?" This is how you stay awake to paddle through your life.

The practice of asking "What is?" allows a person to become skillful at using their attention, know themselves deeply, and stay with their truth in their life, relationships, and sexuality.

It probably goes without saying that to do this kind of check-in with yourself, you need to do it in a place where you are not distracted, especially when you first begin the practice.

Your truth comes from your Inner Person Self. Your truth has the passwords and keys to your Contentment.

Equal Say So
I Count–You Count

Some time ago Tony asked "What if?"

Tony has now arrived at his What Is. He is determined to stay there until he finds peace. When we are awake to What Is, we can paddle our Boat where we want or need to go. Rather than being tossed by our River Minds, we steer our lives with wisdom.

Tony, his wife Jamila, and I are well into our first session when I ask what they hope to accomplish in our work together. They both say "working on our relationship." Specifically, they hope to work on communication and conflict. They both agree that they have been feeling distant and detached with very little joy in their relationship. They take turns detailing the overtime and travel in their work and how little time they have after they get things taken care of in their home.

Tony says, "I feel very lonely." I look at Jamila and she is nodding in agreement.

Even though neither has mentioned sex, I want to bring it up so we can return to it easily.

I continue, "One thing we likely will be talking about in our work is Intimacy. I think of intimacy as a bond that holds people together in a way that sex cannot. I find it helpful when couples have a clear and mutual understanding of intimacy in their relationship.

"I want you to be aware that when you are here in my office, I will be saying 'sex' when I mean 'sex,' and 'intimacy' when I mean 'Intimacy.'

To be a little light-hearted, I add, "I realize that it seems more polite to use the word 'intimacy' for sex, more discreet. However, since I am all about how I can help people be closer, more intimate in their relationship, I take the word 'Intimacy' very seriously!

"So, I bet you know what sex is!" I pause.

Both Tony and Jamila give a little laugh.

"I'll take that as a yes. Let's make sure we are all on the same page, or at least you understand what I mean by the word 'Intimacy.' Because I am going to be using it a lot. So here it is.

"Intimacy is the ability to experience another person while staying with and staying aware of your own experience!

"Sex is not Intimacy. Sex can be intimate, but it is not Intimacy. You can have a sexual experience with another person and barely know that they are there!"

As their guide to what they don't know they don't know, I continue on to a few other guidelines—some helpful hints about our journey.

Tony has already been on the journey to the unknown for some time. He had begun the process to get into couples therapy. At first, when he invited his wife, Jamila, to therapy, she didn't want to come. But Tony did something he didn't often do with Jamila. He persisted and stayed in the uncomfortable, the "awakeness" of his What Is. He firmly insisted that they come to therapy.

Tony's What Is is that he is fed up.

I notice Tony making a quick wipe of his eye. He clears his throat, "That part about holding onto and being aware of your own experience really hit home. I have been getting clearer about what my experience is and what I want and need. I really want to have a relationship where I am an equal partner."

Jamila joins in. "I have noticed that something is happening with Tony. He is changing."

"What have you noticed?" I invite. I watch to see if she heard Tony's want and need that he just shared.

"He listens better and I notice he doesn't get upset when we are talking. He doesn't go all quiet or start explaining himself when we disagree. He now responds with 'I see what you mean' or 'that makes sense.' Which is much more pleasant!"

Nope. She missed it. Although she is commenting about Tony, she shares her own experience of Tony. She doesn't fully acknowledge what Tony just shared. Already Jamila's story and what that story tells about Self is being revealed.

Tony has something he wants to say. I give him the go-ahead.

He stops and takes a breath.

"Jamila, you are the love of my life. We do some things really well, but I don't feel like we are true partners. I really want our marriage to change, for us to be true partners."

Jamila looks disgusted. "Yes, we are partners! What kind of nonsense is that?"

Jamila works at a technology company, a job that brings home considerably more income than Tony's job. She continues. "One of the reasons I keep working at this company is to support you. I work hard and I bring home a lot of money. You get the benefit from my hard work. I should SAY I partner with you!"

I notice the defensive tone and the lack of curiosity about what Tony is saying. I look at him. He seems to notice as well, but Tony has been practicing holding onto his own experience and remains calm.

He says sincerely, "Yes, you do. And I am proud of how talented you are and I feel blessed that you earn such a good living. The part I want you to hear is that my experience is that your work and money are areas that we don't partner in."

Jamila shakes her head, "I can't believe you are saying this."

Still calm, Tony says, "Jamila, my experience is that we don't really partner. If we disagree, I have learned to defer to you. On those occasions where I hang in there because it is important to me, you usually get upset. I notice you often either have the last word or you leave in a huff."

Despite still appearing upset, Jamila asks for examples.

He continues, "Just a simple thing. I will say something I have heard or read, some bit of current news, and you often immediately say, "That's not true!" And then you tell me your opinion. If I do hang in there to discuss the topic, you often continue to reassert your point of view. I have realized that I often walk away from the conversations feeling upset. I am now realizing that you don't ask questions. You just make a pronouncement about what you think, as if I am supposed to think the same way you think."

He continues. Jamila is now looking out the office window. "Even though I am quiet and don't fight and continue the conversation, it does not mean that I agree. What has really happened is that I have given up. I'm not sure you understand that. We don't partner in conversations like this. I don't rock the boat, but you don't treat me like I count, my voice counts."

After a brief silence, he continues with the example of money. "You may think we partner with money, but I don't think you realize that you make financial decisions all the time without my input. On the other hand, you often dismiss my ideas with "We aren't going to do that!" I have to hang pretty tough if

I really want to do something of a bigger spend financially. I feel I have to justify a lot of smaller purchases. And yet you make decisions of big things we are going to buy or not buy all the time. Often, I see you decide on something, take action, or make a purchase without talking to me.

"Another example is you say you are going to do something to save money and then it takes you a long time to do the job, or you don't do it at all. I learned a long time ago not to push back on paying for someone to do work when you say you will do it because you become very upset. Yet I struggle when upkeep and repairs have not been completed because you decided we needed to do them ourselves.

"These are two examples of many. If we are using the definition Dr. Lisa has that intimacy is two people experiencing each other, then we don't have a lot of intimacy. You don't experience me, and I don't hold onto my own Self and what I am experiencing."

Tony looks at Jamila, who is now looking down, silent.

It seems important to let him continue. "I realize that my part in this is that I don't hold onto my experience. I don't speak up from my truth. I always doubt myself when these exchanges happen. That's on me. That's why I am telling you now. I am hoping we can change."

At this point, I am not sure if Jamila and Tony will be able to grow and integrate their Selves into the relationship. I do know that they have a better chance because Tony is waking up and learning to be Responsive to his Self. He is waking up in his Boat, and he is inviting Jamila to wake up, too.

An important point is though it seems that Jamila has the louder voice, she really is not owning her own experience or voice either. When we don't own our own voice, we automatically discount another's voice and try to raise up our own voice.

Tony is practicing the What Is. He started with the "What if?" His "What if?" is "What if my Self and my voice are just as valid as my wife's Self and voice?"

He is Responsive to his Self when he stays with his What Is.

Tony is expressing his voice and his What Is. "I don't feel like my voice counts. I want an equal partnership. I want a partnership with my wife that includes both of our voices."

I am optimistic for this couple. Tony is asking for what I call an "I Count–You Count" agreement. The I Count–You Count agreement is a commitment to full partnership. A couple agrees that both partners have full emotional, mental, and physical ownership. Full ownership. A 100 percent stake in the relationship.

I Count. You Count. It's the important foundation of Intimacy.

The Good Fail
Knee to Knee

Like many of my clients that come to the waiting area and go up the stairs to settle into the chairs for work on their relationship, Diego and Darcey have a mismatched level of sexual desire. It's the number one reason people seek sex therapy in my practice.

Diego and Darcey are back in my office for their fourth session. It so happens that the progression of their homework makes it likely that today they have a good chance of having an Aha about their sex story.

The homework I have assigned them is called the "Knee-to-Knee" exercise. The Knee-to Knee exercise is a practice of What Is.[6]

I usually assign the Knee-to-Knee exercise at the second or third session. Over the years, I have noticed a pattern of how the exercise plays out. It used to surprise me that at the first or second session following starting the assignment of the Knee-to-Knee exercise, the plan would seem to fall apart. Now I expect and welcome that. It is a "good fail."

The Knee-to-Knee exercise, or like the cool kids text "K2K," helps a couple learn how to create an intimate encounter. By the time I present K2K as a homework assignment, the couple has likely heard me repeat my definition of intimacy several times.

Intimacy is the ability to experience another person while staying awake to your own experience.

This simple, fully clothed exercise has an important job to do.

The K2K exercise is a practice of intentionally bringing your whole awake Self to experience your partner's whole awake Self. Bringing everything you got. Just like in Lindy's office, that includes Boat Body, the River Mind, and the

---

6   The Knee to Knee exercise is described in the appendices.

awake Inner Person Self guiding the Boat and where you go on the River. The whole painting.

In addition to practicing "awakeness," the K2K can also help sort out what prevents a couple from bringing their Self to meet their partner's Self.

There are some predictable responses to the homework assignment. One of the most common results is that one or both of the partners minimize clear instructions about actually making sure your knees touch or seem to forget about the assignment altogether.

One partner might confess, "This homework seems silly!" There are quite a few obvious signs of disregard for the instructions that are common. "Oh, we were supposed to take turns?" or "Were we supposed to do it more than once?"

Another trickier response, but no less a sidestep to doing the exercise, is the one where the couple comes back and says, "We do this stuff all the time! We are constantly checking in with each other!" To me this means that they didn't do the exercise because they feel they have mastered this and I just don't understand their advanced capability.

This false sense of ability to be intimate also shows up in couples who are coming in for help to have more consistent and frequent sex, yet tell me they are very good at physical affection. They touch and kiss a lot. Um, really? You do this all the time? What is it you are doing? In other words, in both cases the response shows that they are missing the intimacy part.

When a couple comes back with the "We completed this with no problem—what's next?" result, I know they also missed the point. When I actually walk through it with them, they usually have checked most of the boxes, but cannot tell me what they noticed about themselves or anything new they learned about their partner. They have perfunctorily checked the exercise off the list.

I do try to set each couple up for success.

First, I spend a lot of time laying out what the exercise is practicing. I give examples of the words to use in a K2K encounter. Phrases like "happiest," "the best part of your day," "the highlight that felt good." That could be something like "When did you feel the happiest today?" or "What was the best part of your day?"

I give an example of what is not a K2K encounter; asking "How was your day?" In case you are curious, the first example is an emotional check-in. The second example is a polite ritual, a lovely one, but not an emotional check-in.

Secondly, I am careful to get an out-loud "Yes, I will do this exercise" commitment from both partners.

Oh, and I should mention that I say to every couple, "The only way to fail this exercise is to not do it."

Sometimes I wonder how such otherwise-bright people could have missed the detailed instructions. But not really. I know what throws people off. Why they can't hear the instructions.

It's because of the common sex story of foreplay. The one where if you want sex to go well, it's important to spend some time getting warmed up. Spend time together. Go to dinner. Talk.

Spending time together and having some nice foreplay is cool, but the story underneath the story can be rife with roles, performance, and other validation. To put it another way, you can have all the foreplay, the sexiest foreplay, you can be really revved up and ready for sex, and still be missing the most important part of a sexual experience—you. Your awake Inner Person Self.

I can imagine some thoughts couples have when we are working on K2K and the seemingly strict and over-the-top rules of the exercise. "Yah, yah, I know we need to have a warm-up." "This is way too basic, when do we get to the exciting part?" "Boring; this isn't going to turn me on."

I get it. Even though I tell you that the exercise is practicing showing up with your whole self, you have come to a sex therapist to get help with your sex life. It's what you "know." The usual story is, "If you do foreplay right, the sex will just happen the way it is supposed to happen." Most of us have been imprinted with this story of how sex works.

The Knee-to-Knee exercise is not meant to be foreplay. And while we are at it, the point is not to warm the female up. But that is for another chapter.

This is the "your friend is late, there is no plastic silverware" thing from the chapter on getting to the good part. It's the "yes or no, either or" approach to sex. These couples are not yet asking "What if?." What if showing up with an awake Self is more exciting than foreplay? What if foreplay is not that great because your body is there, but no one (your Self) is home?

The reports after the first round of the Knee-to-Knee exercises vary.

They range from putting off the exercise to the last minute, to doing K2K exactly one time, to feeling that you have done it so well that you are done with the exercise.

Or not doing K2K at all.

That could leave me scratching my head, except I keep in mind the whole point of the exercise is to learn how to bring your Boat, your River, and your awake Inner Person Self to this little meeting with your partner. The best way to learn this kind of thing is to do it or figure out why you didn't do it.

Back to Diego and Darcey. I set up the exercise by laying out the ground rules, the goal, and asking for a volunteer to take the leader role first. Diego raises his hand. I send them on their way to work at home.

*　　*　　*

Three weeks Later. K2K Take One.

Diego and Darcey are back in my office. After the initial greetings and general check-in, I start by saying, "I'm eager to hear how the homework of Knee-to-Knee went for you!"

Diego takes the lead, "I have something that I want to ask you. Dr. Terrell, I don't really get what we are working on here. Darcey has told me many times that she just doesn't think of sex very often. I try to get her to tell me her fantasies and she can't even name one. I feel like we have not begun to address that yet!"

With that opener, I know we have a "fail" for homework. I will need to deliver what I hope will be an Aha to Diego—but not quite yet.

Unknowingly, Diego has just invited me to lead him to a place he doesn't know he doesn't know.

After listening to him, I say, "I hear you, and I think it is an important point. If it is okay with you, I would like to discuss the homework and then return to discuss your concern."

He agrees.

Diego and Darcey go on to report on their Knee-to-Knee homework. And sure enough, they each have led out in the exercise one time. The exercise was assigned three weeks ago. It doesn't add up to rotating every two days.

I give an affirmation anyway. "Good, you gave it a try. Now let's try to learn as much as we can from those two experiences.

"Diego, let's talk about your turn when you invited Darcey to the K2K. What did you notice about yourself?"

He is slow to respond but then hurriedly says, "It was an easy exercise, we don't have problems checking in with our daily lives. I just asked her and then she asked me how my day was."

I persist, "How did you ask, what were the words you actually used?"

I see his upward eyeroll. "Look, Dr. Terrell, you asked us to do something we have no problem doing and we did it. I realize you have to start us somewhere to improving our sex life, but foreplay isn't the problem we have here."

I get it. This feels like sending your child to pre-school when the kid can already read. It feels like an insult. Duh, everyone knows that foreplay is important!

Ah, there is that pesky foreplay part of the sex story.

But it is wrong to think that I am assigning a "touchy-feely-female-friendly" way of easing into, a warming-up foreplay. That is a tired old song of warming up the female to get them ready for sex. In this case, it shows another story of sex. If you go there, it is a dead-end. The K2K has just revealed the story. The story of why sex isn't working.

The K2K is great at flushing this story out in the open.

I say it out loud, very firmly: "The Knee-to-Knee is not there to help you do better foreplay."

At any rate, we have confirmed what the couple "knows." I think it is likely that most people need to start there. But the Knee-to-Knee is always inviting you to a place that you don't know you don't know.

I continue, "The Knee-to-Knee exercise is like a kindergarten to help you learn Intimacy."

With that, I ask Darcey to talk about what she noticed about the two times they did K2K. I am relieved when Darcey, who has been silent up to this point, speaks right up.

"I really like the Knee-to-Knee homework! I don't think we are doing it completely right, we only did it twice. Yet, with this agreement and plan, I feel more hopeful about our relationship. It gives me something to work with. When it's my turn, I know I have two days. Diego can't invite, it's my gig. I also like it when it is his turn, I don't feel anxious that maybe there is something I need to be doing."

Surprisingly, she continues, "The actual exercise feels so good. I get those minutes of his undivided attention. Holding hands is nice and by the looking at each other I feel like we are paying attention to each other."

I look over at Diego. He too surprises me by saying, "Yes, that is really a good feeling, the holding hands and focusing on each other feels good for me, too." I mentally give him some points for sticking with the discussion even though he is skeptical about the K2K.

Darcey is on a roll. "I do wish Diego would be more into it. I had to remind him how to ask the questions because he just blurted out, 'How was your day?'"

"The other thing that I want to confirm is that we are supposed to let no more than two days go by, right?" I nod. "When it was his turn, he waited five days and this last time it's been a week."

Diego readjusts in his chair and looks annoyed. It seems that he can't understand why he is being called out about such minor details.

Diego is being confronted with something he never imagined: not doing well in sex therapy.

Darcey, on the other hand, is awake and is coming alive. She is on her way. Turns out, she's going to lead Diego to a place he didn't know he didn't know.

I watch as she presents Diego with his "What if? Aha!"

She shakes Diego awake by saying, "I know this is a minor detail, but I was really hurt when you went past the time. I felt like you didn't really want to spend time with me. Like you don't really desire me if it wasn't going to include sex. When you did ask so carelessly, I was disappointed that you just wanted to get it over with!"

I look at Diego.

Diego, who came in professing that his desire for his beautiful partner was so strong and he was feeling so totally undesired, was the one who made his partner feel undesired. Diego's face shows that he is doing that exact calculation. He is alert and paying attention now.

What a delightful twist in the story. I remember when I led Diego and Darcey up the stairs to begin sex therapy, Darcey said she was very disappointed in herself, that she just didn't think of sex, and really had to make an effort to meet Diego for sex. Her discouragement and anxiety showed in her face. What would the sex therapist ask her to do?

Since everyone is now awake, we return to talking about the exercise.

I take the couple back through their experiences. "How did it feel when he invited you? How did it feel when she invited you? How did it feel to share the emotional highs and lows of your day?"

We discuss at length the ways that they could have experienced each other in this simple exercise.

We review the physical contact, mental contact, and emotional contact. How to make contact. How to experience your partner while you hold onto your own experience. Showing up to the K2K like Lindy's painting. The Person in the Boat on the River who is wide awake, conscious, and present.

Darcey shares that she feels excited by knowing that she could get this time with Diego. She adds that she has been thinking that if she could have Diego's undivided attention more often, that would feel great. She has started to think about taking this feeling of togetherness into their next sexual encounter. She says she thinks it would be good for her to invite Diego to "the paying attention to each other" and that she could use this to initiate sex and not wait for him to come to her.

There is movement from Diego's chair, but this time he is not annoyed. His facial expression has relaxed and he is looking intently over at Darcey. I think he is beginning to understand that we are working on sex. Darcey has shown him a desire for Intimacy and how that fits into sex.

I want to make sure I am seeing correctly.

I turn to Diego. "Now about that question you had when we started session."

"I'm good. Darcey has answered it."

He has had his Aha. He has made the connection between this silly, fully clothed exercise and his story of sex that isn't working.

Diego is surprised that Darcey invited him to the exercise and began to speak about the next sexual encounter. She is energized and positive.

Diego's surprise showed his story of sex. He thought he had the sex thing all wrapped up, and that Darcey with the low desire needed lots of sex help. Darcey had fully agreed with this. But in moving to a Kindergarten level of Intimacy, it was discovered that he was behind in knowing the letters of contact.

Now Darcey can let go of her story that she's just not as sexual and invite Diego to a new story. A Sexuality that incorporates sex and Intimacy.

It was a good fail!

Uncomfortable What Ifs

Awake During Sex?

Davis asked a surprising and uncomfortable "What if?" and it brought him and his wife Ava to the What Is of their sex life.

I'm on the phone with Ava for an initial consultation. She starts with, "Davis and I are having a problem with the intimate part of our life. We've had a good marriage—fifty-six years. We raised three successful children. We have grandchildren and are very proud of our family! We've had our ups and downs, but have been pretty happy all these years. Until the last three months."

She continues, "Davis came home from a golf trip he takes every year with his brother and a college friend, and he told me he wanted to have an open marriage.

"This has been heartbreaking to me. I have always trusted Davis. I always thought we had a great marriage and an okay sex life. But this has broadsided me. Now we are arguing, and I don't recognize him. He is saying things about what he wants to try and telling me how unsatisfying sex has been all these years. If he's not going to be happy, and it ends our marriage, how am I going to find a partner at my age?

"We have tried to talk about our sex life. I feel like we have done pretty good with sex. I have always been receptive when Davis wanted sex and we are still having sex once or twice a week. I think that is pretty good for people our age.

"Davis keeps saying there is more that he wants for our sex life. He is especially focused on this because of a conversation with his golf buddies. They talked about open marriages. Since then, he has not been able to nor does he want to drop it. When I ask him why this appeals to him, he says that he has been disappointed over the years that I would have sex with him because 'he' wanted it. He keeps coming back to saying, 'Not once did you approach me wanting sex.'"

*　　*　　*

Davis and Ava start sex therapy. They tell me about their day-to-day life at home, their business they run together, and the family celebrations they host. They seem to have a working, functioning partnership. I notice their "I Count–You Count" conversation style even as they introduce themselves.

I ask them to tell me about their hopes for our work together.

Ava starts with the discussion they had about open marriage. "I would like us to figure out how to have sex that satisfies Davis. I feel like he is downplaying all the good years we have had. We are still having sex. I think it is unfair that at our age he is wanting to trade me in as if I am too old. He's getting old, too. I want to figure out how to get Davis the kind of sex he needs because I think our sex is normal."

Davis answers, "Yes, we have sex, but it isn't very good sex." He says it isn't good because Ava doesn't really participate all that much. She hasn't been interested in an orgasm for a long time now, and she won't tolerate foreplay or much kissing. "As soon as I have climaxed, she gets up immediately, goes to the bathroom to clean up, and puts her pajamas on. I don't think we are having sex; I feel like only I am having sex."

Ava interjects. "That's not fair. I enjoy it. I just don't need to have an orgasm."

I see that they may have a good partnership in their marriage overall, but sex is like a closed bridge and there is a wide river of stories between them.

I ask Davis, "What's your hope for our work together?"

"I want us to enjoy sex together. I want to find a way for Ava to enjoy sex. I think right now, it is just a chore she does. The reason I asked her about open marriage is because I love her and everything else about our lives is good. Since it seems like she doesn't want the same kind of sex I want, I thought counseling might be something that would help."

What the couple has shared is helpful. Davis had started with a "What if?" What if we opened our marriage up to have sex with other people? It also confirms that Ava and Davis have a very limited viewpoint of sex. Although they seem to enjoy each other and have a functioning life partnership, they do not partner with sex.

In fact, when it comes to their sex life, they don't really understand what a goldmine is hidden away in their relationship. I will show them how to connect, how to build a bridge to get to the good part.

After a lively discussion and introduction to the concept of building a bridge of connection, I introduce the K2K exercise.

I will need to come back to several points, but for now I can feel them following closely with the ideas I am presenting. I assign the Knee-to-Knee exercise.

*   *   *

Three weeks later, Davis and Ava have returned and they are in an upbeat mood.

Davis starts the recap of their experiences. "I really like the Knee-to-Knee. At first, I thought it was way too basic. Ava and I are together most of every day and we talk a lot throughout the day. Even so, I am seeing the huge difference it makes to stop everything and face each other, hold hands, and focus on your partner's experience. Those three minutes are very powerful."

Ava barely lets Davis finish before she reports how much she "loved" the Knee-to Knee.

"I think the most important part for me—that felt so great—was how it felt when Davis invited me. When you assigned it, I thought that it was so basic that Davis would never bother with it. I was surprised when he told me at breakfast that he would like to do the Knee-to-Knee that evening. And I was even more surprised that right after supper he invited me and showed me where he had set up chairs."

True to my first observation that this couple has good partnering skills, they have taken to the K2K and are experiencing another level of partnership Intimacy with their emotional experiences.

During the final minutes of the session, Ava looks at Davis and says, "I want you to know that I feel really close to you right now. After the first week of us doing the homework, I started to think that I wanted sex. Now we are here after three weeks and I feel that even stronger. When I think of how close I feel to you, it makes me think of sex. Don't be surprised if I come to you and invite you to sex!"

At first glance, it may seem from the experiences of this couple that the point of the exercise is to give Ava the emotional support she needs in order to get her to want to have sex. Especially since Ava liked it. I do see that happen with quite a few couples.

However, whether you are male, female, or non-binary, waking the person in the Boat on the River is the same process. The awakening of a Self helps you start to move from and not rely on the story of Self you get from roles, performance, and external validation. The more you move into and sit with What Is, the more Responsive to Self and Awake you become in your River Mind and Boat Body .

The important thing about the K2K is practicing being awake. You are awake when you commit and plan to make deliberate contact with your partner. You are awake when you communicate your desire to meet your partner through the keeping of the commitment and the invitation to the partner. You are awake when you come to the moment with full attention to your partner and their experience. You are awake when you are able to speak about your emotional experience.

*　　*　　*

Their next report showed that they both felt they had made progress. Davis shared with pride that Ava had initiated sex more than he had. "It feels so great to have Ava invite me!"

At this point, my thoughts begin to turn to my "less is more" plan. This is my philosophy that when a couple starts fully partnering and their intimacy has been energized, I let go and stop actively supporting and directing their activities. It's like a parent teaching a child to ride a bike. You start by holding the bike and jogging behind helping to keep the child balanced. At some point, you let go. At first the child does not realize you let go because they have learned to balance and are riding their bike.

It is looking like it may be time to let go. They are no longer wrangling with the "open" marriage idea at all. They have re-engaged and re-energized their sex life. I write "graduation?" on my session notes to remind me to check their readiness next time.

I am happy for couples who graduate after a few sessions. Some do.

*　　*　　*

However, the next session shows early graduation isn't for this couple.

Ava is very upset. She and Davis had been talking last week and Ava had enthused that they had a whole new sex life and looked at Davis. She noticed something weird in his facial expression. She asked him, "Hasn't this therapy been great?" And followed it with, "I feel so different, I love sex now!"

Davis surprised her by saying, "Yes, I'm glad that we have started to make progress!"

This shocked and upset Ava. She shared how depressing it was to have him say that. "I have never initiated sex in our whole marriage. Now, I am genuinely and excitedly initiating sex, and we are having sex a lot, and all he can say is we have started to make progress."

Davis nods in agreement. Ava doesn't look at him and she gets louder. "I have given this my all and it isn't good enough. I don't understand why you would say we still have work to do. I don't think I'm ever going to be what you watch in your porn; I won't and I don't ever want to!" I notice she has thrown him under the bus by announcing this previously undisclosed information. He looks uncomfortable. She continues. "Maybe we should give up now!"

I look at Davis again. He says, "Ava, honey, I am enjoying our sex. I'm just saying there is more I think we could enjoy."

I invite him to say more. He has a list. "Sex seems like something she likes to check off of her to-do list. Once we have agreed we will have sex, or more like when she says, 'Let's have sex,' we get right to it. No kissing, no lead-up. Although it is enjoyable, we do it the same way every time. Immediately after sex, she gives me a kiss and quickly gets up to put her pajamas on. Other than her inviting me to sex, nothing has changed. It still feels like just I am having sex."

Ava quickly responds. "I enjoy sex and I'm glad we are having more of it, but I don't like to be naked. It does not feel good to me. I feel more relaxed in my pajamas." She repeats, "We are having more sex than we ever have, even when we were first married. We are pretty healthy compared to many people our age. I just don't think you are ever going to be satisfied. I'm tired of this. Maybe you should go find someone who satisfies you!"

I now realize that I have been too quick to think of hands-off here. Hold on, we are doing a U-turn. I see it now. We are still in passive, non-intimate territory. The Knee-to-Knee has not revealed the "What if?" about sex to Ava yet.

They are not yet where they need to be in order to evolve their sex life. Immediately getting the pajamas back on is a clue that Ava is not awake in her painting.

My work thus far with this couple was to get them to deliberately create a "bridge" by using the "3Ds of contact." Doing the K2K exercise with deliberate emotional, mental, and physical connection. They took to that quickly. They demonstrated the skills to experience each other. I understand now that they quickly disconnect into their own worlds when they start sex. A common pattern for many.

When it comes to sex, they are asleep in their Boat Body on their River Mind—especially Ava. She is either ready for sex or not. Yes or no. If it is a yes, it is a limited and passive experience. She directs the sexual experience. "Yes, I will have a climax" or "No, just you tonight." She experiences "enjoyable sex" in a narrow and train-track way. Ava is not awake during sex. Her Boat Body goes wherever her River Mind pulls her.

Davis practices "Closed" sex with his near daily porn experiences. Porn often reinforces the habits of what I called "Closed" sex in the Arousal Pathway.[7]

During sex, this couple is missing something. They are both missing. They are both asleep. Although the orgasm eventually awakens them fully, it is short lived. In contrast to the K2K experience, neither Ava nor Davis shows up for sex.

Ava and Davis are not at all unusual.

---

7   The "Closed Sexual Arousal Pathway" is discussed and illustrated in the upcoming chapter "How to Do Sex."

Naked Holding
Staying Present. Staying Awake.

I sent Ava and Davis, a couple in their seventies, home to practice experiencing each other in a new way.

They were to crawl into bed together. Although getting into bed at the same time was usually a signal that they would have sex, I invited them to try something different. "Keep your pajamas and undies on. Just hang out and enjoy the holding and being held. This isn't about sex, this is about what you experience holding each other."

Though initially very reluctant, Ava said she would give it a try. Davis said he would, too.

They are back today, and I ask about the What Is of their experience. My hope is that they have experienced an open connection like they practiced in K2K. And they have.

"What did you notice as you were holding each other?" I ask.

Ava says happily, "It was such a relief not to think about sex. It felt really great to be held. As I was holding, I really noticed how good his skin felt. And after that first one I couldn't wait for Davis to invite me back. I like this 'pajama holding' thing!"

Davis follows. "I was amazed how relaxed I felt. And she was relaxed, too. I could feel it. We did it for about twenty minutes. We just quietly and unhurriedly stayed there and talked. It felt good."

A good report.

I want to keep the momentum going. I announce the next assignment as the "Naked or Pajamas Holding exercise."

Davis speaks up. "Ava, would you feel better if I just let you call the naked part for a while?"

She smiles. "That would be good. I'm still anxious, but I do want to push myself. I'm just not sure I can enjoy nakedness."

Davis and Ava's work continues. When they come back for the next session, they have done several Pajamas Holding exercises, some K2Ks, and one Naked Holding exercise. Ava was brave and invited Davis to that one.

She shares her concerns. "I just couldn't relax. We kept to five minutes this time. I'm just so worried that Davis is getting upset about no sex. I wish I could go faster. When are you going to tell us we need to have sex?"

"It's up to you two," I say. "However, I don't really think it's a good idea to have sex again until you feel comfortable being naked together. Not as a way to start sex, but as a way to savor how your naked body feels and experience how your partner's naked body feels. It's like you practice comfort and enjoyment of your nakedness."

I look to Davis for some back-up that he isn't getting angry about sex.

He looks at Ava. "Well, I am missing sex, especially after we went through that time of having more sex than we have ever had. But I want us to do the work. I think you will enjoy learning how to do this. I will enjoy learning how to do this.

"And as for us not having sex for a few weeks, and I am saying *weeks,* not months," he says like it's a joke. I know it's not really a joke. "We have the rest of our lives to enjoy sex and it will be better if we are naked and like being naked together."

Davis is doing just fine.

Ava and Davis work to get comfortable and enjoy the Naked Holding exercise. They will go on to the Yellow Light Encounters, where they will practice building an Intimacy Bridge and staying with the What Is. We will work on Pleasure, Open Lovemaking skills, and Erotic Flow.

Davis had asked the uncomfortable "What if we should have an open marriage?" I had asked Ava the uncomfortable "What if you showed up and participated in sex in a way that felt good to you?"

The "What ifs" enabled this couple to wake up to the skill of What Is. And just as importantly, the What Is of being present together.

Code Zombie
Relationship Resuscitation

I have lost some clients in my relationship and sexuality therapy work. By lost, I mean I did not help them.

I have made mistakes. I have said things that I wish I hadn't. When I realize that I wasn't helpful to a client or couple, I feel sad and disappointed. If I have the opportunity, I apologize. I realize I am an imperfect therapist. I work to learn to be more trustworthy and skillful in guiding my fellow Boaters. I know I can't help everybody, yet I will do my best.

A few years into practicing sex therapy, I realized there was one kind of couple that was extra challenging to me: the "Zombified" couple. I don't want to make another mistake and call these clients "zombies." I do think it is helpful to see that their sex life has zombified their relationship. These couples don't get anywhere near asking "What if?" Instead, their understanding about themselves and their situation is a spinning merry-go-round of Latent, Performance, and Validation stories. They spin 'round and 'round until they can't see anything but whether they have sex or not. These are stories that are about the Outside Self. You can always tell an Outside Self story because it is always ends in a yes or no ending.

Stories like "physical touch is my love language, so when we don't have sex, I don't feel loved." "Men need sex, women need the emotions." "My partner is not a sexual person." "My partner is too sexual. "I'm a highly sexual person!"

Do you have enough sex? Yes or no.

No, there aren't many "What ifs" these couples ask. They will continue to ask yes or no questions until neither one of them feel good about their relationship.

In my effort to be the best therapist I can be, I now have what I call a Code Zombie. It's what I write on my pad of paper as soon as I see it in session. The idea of the Code Zombie came from my experiences as a bedside nurse calling "Code Blues" in the hospital.

When a person is very ill or injured, they are admitted to the hospital to get treatment. Sometimes the patients are so ill or injured that they are close to dying. When you walk into a patient's room and they are not breathing, you "call a Code Blue." When a patient's heart stops beating, and the green line on the monitor goes flat, you push the Code Blue button on the wall.

When the overhead announcement is called, hospital personnel are trained to drop everything and rush to the patient to save their life.

Code Blue 2 North Room 2124,
Code Blue 2 North Room 2124,
Code Blue 2 North Room 2124.

Three times, so that the Code Team knows exactly where to go.

The team quickly gets to the patient to do everything they can to save their life. Quick and decisive, they have practiced and trained. A Code Blue is a patient's last chance to come back from death.

Like a Code Blue in the hospital, my therapy rescue technique helps me kick into gear quickly so that I can prevent as many failed sessions as I can. As soon as I confirm that one of the partners is unconscious in the conversation we are starting in therapy, I know it's an emergency. I "call" a Code Zombie.

Of course, I don't have an overhead page or a team to come running. Instead, I move forward in my chair and my focus. I take a deep breath and slide forward in my chair to ground my feet. Like a Code Blue, I only have a few minutes to bring back the couple to partner again.

When someone calls themselves "highly" sexual, it is usually the title of their story of sex. You will remember that we have defined Sexuality as the stories we have about sex and what those stories tell us about Self. It means that sex is important to their sense of who they are—their Outside Self. They feel good about themselves when sex is good, and anxious when sex doesn't go well. They have sexualized their story of self. They are deeply asleep. Their eyes are open, but they are not awake. They act like they are zombies.

Highly sexualized couples have two defining characteristics. One partner actually calls themself "highly sexual," and the couple has sex almost daily. Daily sex isn't the problem. The daily need for sex to help yourself or your partner feel good and okay is.

*   *   *

Warren and Maria were a couple that didn't present as in dire need of relationship resuscitation at first. Warren emailed me to set up a phone consultation.

"Please help, my wife was sexually abused as a child and I think it is affecting our sex life. She doesn't ever really want to have sex."

"What are you noticing?" I ask.

"Maria just doesn't think about sex. It's not important to her. I get put last on the list."

I notice he uses "I" interchangeably with "sex." A sign that he is not awake.

"It's gotten so bad, that I have these thoughts in my head and ask if she's seeing someone else. We argue about that a lot."

We set an appointment. Of course, I don't say anything about what he has already revealed about himself, but I take note. I will be on alert when I meet the couple.

*　　*　　*

The next week, I meet Warren and Maria for the first time in the waiting area. When I see them, I instantly feel myself take a quick breath in surprise and a pause.

Maria doesn't seem to fit the picture Warren had painted on our introductory phone call.

They are seated picture perfect on the couch. Looking relaxed and confident. They are beautiful. They both are super put-together. Wearing stylish clothes, rocking beautiful hair, and smelling expensively wonderful.

I notice that Maria does not hesitate and is the first to stand up and offer her hand.

"Hi, I'm Maria, and this is my husband, Warren!"

A back-and-forth conversation flows easily as we go up the stairs to my office and settle in for session.

Then there is an obvious shift.

The lightness of the conversation suddenly drops off to a polite silence.

I have the floor. I begin as always with some questions about jobs, kids, and pets. I take note that Warren and Maria have shifted to short and clipped answers. They are not elaborating.

This is not unusual, as the stress and emotional weight of being "in sex therapy" settles in the room.

I begin the work in earnest by asking my pretend-not-pretend question about their relationship.

"What would you tell a trusted friend about how you feel about your marriage?"

Warren doesn't let me finish my sentence before he jumps in to answer. He doesn't answer the question, but tells his story. Maria is quiet, her face blank.

Sexual activity, lots of it, is a big part of the story he shares. He says that they have sex just about every day. But that isn't enough. He wants Maria to want to have sex. He is always the initiator. He wants her to initiate sex, to dress sexy, and to show that she is attracted to him.

He is not shy about stating that he is a man and he needs to feel like a man. As he tells his sex story, I notice that on the one hand, he is proud of Maria. He comments frequently on her looks and how she is dressed. "I mean, look at her. What man wouldn't be turned on? She's hot!" On the other hand, he takes what seems to be a seething, barely hidden anger and keeps returning to Maria's need to deal with her past. "I just think you haven't dealt with your past and it is ruining our life."

I let him talk for a few minutes and then interrupt and thank him. I assure him that I will hear him out. I take back the leadership of the session. I need to hear from Maria. She has changed from the elegant and confident presence in the lobby to not moving and looking down at the carpet.

Hearing from Maria is tough. When I turn to her and ask her what would she tell a trusted friend about how she feels about her marriage, there is a long silence.

I let the room be silent. I can tell Warren wants to talk and he is barely holding it in. I look at him to give the message, "Let it be silent." He holds. More silence.

Maria is slumped in her chair. I realize she is unresponsive. She is alive, but not really here in the discussion. She does not have an emotional heartbeat. She is silent.

Like a flat green line on a heart monitor that causes a nurse to call, "CODE BLUE!" Maria's silence calls, "CODE ZOMBIE!" in my thoughts.

It is a critical event. Time is of the essence. If I can't get Maria "breathing" and "awake," this couple will likely never be a happy and healthy couple or return to work on their sex life.

I quickly scribble "Code Z" on my note pad, set it aside, and start relationship resuscitation.

Like basic life-saving training, the first thing to look for is if the airway is open. Is something blocking the breath? Can Maria get air?

To clear Maria's airway, we have to help Warren not take up all the air in the room by talking for her. I immediately start to give her some of my breath, and invite her heart, her side of the line, to become part of the conversation.

I want to help Maria find her voice.

I go to the whiteboard and hurriedly write a list twice and draw a line through it. It is the "I Count–You Count" Dialog graph.

It's an all-or-nothing move.

I Count—You Count Dialog

Me		You
THOUGHTS		THOUGHTS
EMOTIONS, FEELINGS		EMOTIONS, FEELINGS
NEEDS		NEEDS
REQUESTS		REQUESTS
WANTS, DESIRES		WANTS, DESIRES

The list represents her side of the line and his. The line through the middle is important, because in this couple's sex life, it has been missing. For partnerships to be happy and healthy, both sides of the line have to count.

I Count. You Count.

My rescue attempt, my asking her to talk about her side of the line, does not immediately start Maria. In fact, Warren jumps in with, "I thought we were here to talk about sex!"

If Warren was on a monitor, we would see that he isn't doing well either. He is also barely aware of his emotions. He seems alive because he can talk about sex. And he talks about sex a lot. It's about the only thing he talks to Maria about. His River Mind, the current of his thoughts, has him spinning around and around.

His story of sex is telling me about his viewpoint of himself. Later I will help Warren discover that contrary to being all together sexually, he feels like crap because, in his words, he's "not desirable enough for Maria to want to have sex with."

This highly sexual guy sees himself as having arrived. He feels good about sex from his end, if only his partner would cooperate. Because of his story of sex, he cannot fathom how this is going to fix Maria sexually. He is entirely missing the line and the point of the list.

It isn't a given that when I offer the shock—I ask Maria to talk about her emotions, thoughts, needs, wants, and desires—she will be able to do it.

I see Warren's growing anxiety, but I also give him a shock by saying, "I think it's important for Maria to talk right now." It's my "stand clear" message to Warren.

An important part of a sex encounter is the ability to tune in to and understand your partner's experiences, to tune in to your partner. In this zombified relationship, the experience is all Warren's. He's absorbed and drifting in his own experience of his River Mind.

Warren and Maria can't hear each other when they are talking about sex, so it's no surprise they don't experience each other while having sex.

He doesn't make contact with Maria during sex. Maria isn't even in contact with herself during sex. She has shut down to protect herself and get Warren what he needs.

I look at Maria. I'm not looking for much. I just want her to say something about herself.

The first thing she says confirms for me that my emergency response is starting to work.

"It is true that I had some things happen to me when I was in high school. I may still need to do some work on that, but I don't think that experience is ruining our sex life. I am not ruining our sex life. We have sex every day, and on the weekends and trips more than that."

Warren starts to talk. She looks at him and says, "It's my turn. I did not interrupt you when you talked."

She continues, "I would like for us to do something as a couple that doesn't involve sex. Yes, I have started to turn you down. It has taken me years to be able to do that. And I think I need to do that."

She pauses to look at me, as if to make sure I have her back.

She has begun to share her side of the line. Maria is breathing. She is waking and becoming Responsive to her Inner Person Self.

My vision and hope for this couple is that Warren will also begin to wake up. I want to guide them not just to have sex, but show up for their sex life.

Email

Needing Sex

If you get an email from me, the "Dr. Lisa Terrell at Sensovi Institute" me, you will notice the signature says that I am a "Relationship and Sexuality" specialist. It has always been important to make a statement about the relationship part. This is not because I think everyone should be monogamous or should get married before they have sex.

No, it is because I am always looking for the story of Self in any relationship or sexual experience. I don't think it's helpful to separate relationships and sex, because in both areas, your story always includes your relationship with your own Self.

The word "sexuality" is like a wallflower at a party. While sex is the one people congregate around and are interested in—the life of the party—Sexuality goes unnoticed.

There is a pretty common idea that your sexuality is who or what you are attracted to. Although how you identify yourself sexually is part of your stories of Sexuality, your Sexuality is much richer and deeper than that. Here's a definition that might be more helpful.

Sexuality is a collection of the stories we have about sex and what those stories tell us about our Self.

Your Sexuality comes from your stories. For good or for bad. Your unique story is always the key to moving on or getting rid of a problem with sex. The more I have worked with people and their sex lives and lack of sex life, the more I appreciate how important the individual's unique understanding of sex is.

For these reasons, although I am a certified sex therapist, I don't use the phrase "sex therapist" or "sex therapy" very much. I really don't like it. It seems misleading to me.

I use the word "Sexuality" more than the word "sex." The word "sex" can get so overused, boring, sterile, and tiring. The word "Sexuality" is endlessly fascinating. At least to me.

The story you tell and accept about yourself and sex can be misery-making or it can become a source of contentment. The trouble is that there are some widely accepted sex ideas that are like a counterfeit twenty-dollar bill, or a deep fake YouTube video. They don't pass. Not with the yellow marker or the analyzing software.

Let's start with this one.

The story of "I need sex!" It is a biggie!

The statement can pass as legit. A normal human need. A part of the human experience. Sex keeps you healthy. It's what you sign up for with monogamy. You deserve pleasure. Common knowledge. Research shows.

"I need sex" is a story you tell yourself about yourself and sex. It seems right. Duh! Harmless, even.

It can feel like you found an important fact for your sex life. "When my partner touches me, I feel loved. So of course, that's why I want and need sex so much!"

"Passion is the glue that holds my partner and me together. Without sex, we are just roommates!"

"A man's body needs sex."

"A woman gets bitchy when she doesn't have sex."

The need for sex presents a strong argument. It's biology, after all.

Yet I ask "What is the person's story about how their Self is helped or hurt by those needs?" There is always a story people tell themselves about their Self and sex.

What does the story of needing sex tell you about your Self?

Chess
Waking Up

As we look at the Sexuality story of needing sex, it may be helpful to think of Sexuality as like the Queen piece of the chess board.

Chess has been around for a very long time. Let's say that sex is the "King." In chess, the point of the game is the pursuit of the King. At first glance, it may seem that it is the most powerful piece on the chess board. In life, the pursuit of sex and having sex is often seen as what you need to feel fulfilled and happy. I think there is something more powerful than sex. Your Sexuality, the "Queen," has all the power.

I was intrigued to find out that the Queen piece is a modern adaptation. The piece used to be called a "counselor" and could only move one space at a time. Through the many years of chess, the counselor became a Queen. She was given the ability to move any number of spaces at a time. The creation of the Queen made it the most valuable piece in chess. The King is important, but to play the game with success you really need to use the power of your Queen. Our Sexuality is more powerful than the sex we have. It serves as a counselor for our life, if we let it.

If you need sex to feel loved, for physical release, for mental health, physical health, quality of life, or to keep your partner happy—I believe you. It is normal to feel this way about sex, and most of us do.

Think of these "needs" as stories about yourself. What if there was something more awake, steadier, and more reliable and contentment-making than getting needs met?

The key here is that your sexual experiences are only part of your Sexuality. There is also your ability to experience another human being—your Intimacy skills. The most wise and powerful chess move of your Sexuality is to go from needing sex to wanting to make Intimate contact, experiencing another human. It's like a "Queen's Gambit. The "Queen's Gambit" is an opening move in chess whereby you let a pawn be taken in order to gain the advantage of controlling the center of the board. Likewise, although stopping to make an Intimate connection with a partner may seem to sacrifice the spontaneous passion energy, it actually supports sexual energy for the whole experience, not just for arousal. In fact, it could be said that Intimate connection with yourself and a partner is the point of your Sexuality. Needing sex is the go-to move we know until we advance in our understanding and skill. Need sex for what?

We don't need sex to define Self. That is a story. We don't have a part of us that is missing, a piece to find in sexual experiences to help us feel good about ourselves. Self, the Person in the Boat, is always there in our Inner space of awareness. This inner place is where we watch our River Minds and tune in to our Boat Bodies. When we open our eyes and understand and begin to be present, steering and paddling with our attention so that we don't get swept away and sedated by our River Mind, we find a new peace, presence, and wisdom. That is the missing piece. An awake present Inner Person Self.

This is where the stories of your sexuality are important. What strategy do you have if though you need sex, you can't get it? Or what do you do if you really don't need sex, but your partner does? Your Sexuality has the answer. The queen and counselor of your mind is inviting you to go beyond needing sex to feel satisfied and content. It's about having sex because you are content inside you, not using sex to find happiness and satisfaction.

This all reminds me of an episode on a TV show that illustrates this idea of not needing something to get content, but choosing something because you are content.

The beginning of the pandemic in 2020 found my husband and me working our way through the eleven seasons of the TV show *M*A*S*H* in the evenings. It is the story of a Mobile Army Surgical Hospital in the Korean War. This comedy-style drama tackles the tough realities of doctors and nurses on the front lines of the war and is based on a true story.

Helicopters and buses would bring wounded soldiers from the front lines. The doctors and nurses had a hard, bloody, grim, and exhausting job. They called their work "meatball surgery" because they had to patch up a wounded soldier in the quickest way to save the most lives. As one doctor said, "I had to take this soldier's leg, in order to save the life of the kid waiting in triage." Horrifying.

Heavy drinking was a pass-the-time activity to fill the down hours and mute the miseries of war. On one episode, Pierce, who was the lead surgeon, was joking around with his doctor friend and tentmate BJ. They usually drank together. One time they went to the camp bar, and the bartender noted that Pierce had the largest unpaid tab of the camp, meaning he drank the most in the camp. There was a discussion of who drank the most. In a sudden twist of the banter, Pierce suddenly announced he would go for one week without drinking.

The week unfolded with the whole camp rooting for him to make the full week. They even supported him when he was being annoying, like bragging with a superior air about how much better he felt by not drinking.

Toward the end of that week, they had a heavy batch of injured soldiers delivered by bus and helicopter. After performing surgery for more than twenty-four hours, everyone met in the officers' club for a drink to unwind.

Surprising everyone, Pierce ordered a drink. The head nurse, Major Houlihan, said, "You only have one day left, don't ruin it now!" Pierce responded with "I really need a drink!" The whole group erupted noisily with everyone talking at once. Some argued "Leave him alone" and others shouted "Come on, man, you can do it!"

Looking shocked at the protests from both sides, Pierce paused with the drink in hand. Everyone was silent. He then said, "You know what? I am not going to drink. I will be back when I don't need it!" And he quickly left the bar.

In that moment, Pierce moved from needing a drink. It was a wake-up moment. It meant that he decided to look at his pain and the horror and work through it a different way rather than put himself back to sleep with alcohol. His Self clearly saw the River of his Mind and tuned into being present in the uncomfortable moment to the situation. His awake Self acted to direct his life. He decided not to get swept away to a stupor in the pain of the moment.

How did Pierce, with a drink in his hand, put that drink down and walk away? He looked and saw his drinking story. He felt pain and distress in the work and horrors of war, and the way to feel better was to heavily sedate himself with alcohol—make the pain go away. Only, drinking didn't make the horror go away. It only hooked him into more alcohol, more often. He had a wake-up moment when he saw the harm in drifting through the war under heavy emotional sedation.

It was his Inner Person Self, the captain of his Boat Body, that was aware of his River Mind, that directed himself through dangerous terrain. His awake Self picked up a paddle, and he paddled his Boat out of the pull of his River Mind, and the current that kept him adrift.

Couples and the Canary

River Story

If zombies are intense because they require immediate emergency measures, Canary Couples are the most challenging for me.

Canary Couples convince me of their couple story. My problem is that I ignore the canary. I keep buying into their story, ignoring my What Is with them.

You likely know that miners used to take small birds in cages down in the mines in order to be alerted if the air became deadly. Deadly, as in the miners could die if their underground tunnel filled with a deadly gas. I'm sure you have also heard the phrase "canary in the mine" to describe something that should be taken as a warning sign.

Although my skill in paying attention to the canary I bring with me has improved, I have at times completely missed when the poor bird keeled over.

In retrospect, I usually could remember that the bird was acting funny, was lethargic, or was not giving so much as a chirp. Now, I work to look at the canary regularly and to believe myself that the bird isn't acting right.

These couples that I call Canary Couples have several things that I find very challenging.

For starters, they often don't seem like they are as fragile as they really are.

Another common sign is that they come to work on their sex life. Most of them have not had sex for years.

I have found that the trickiest issue for me is it seems like these couples usually have a big secret. Secrets like porn, paid sex, online fantasy, gambling, money secrets, long-term secret relationships, drugs, alcohol, and sexual activity.

A secret can be the missing piece that connects the whole story together to make complete sense.

Rita and Steve were a Canary Couple. Before I tell you their story, I want to remind you that this isn't a real couple but a common story created from many similar couples. Many kinds of Canary Couples have come under my watch. I didn't know that I didn't know about this "canary behavior" at first. I learned through painful "Aha" moments that came from mistakes and blunders. I have helped Canary Couples. Some greatly, some a little bit, and some not at all.

Rita and Steve

When I invite Rita and Steve to sit in my therapy chairs, I notice that they have an easy manner with me and with each other. They talk positively about their daughters. They give each other very generous compliments. Steve says Rita is a great mom. Rita says Steve is the best cook she knows. It seems like they really like their lives, a very canary-like characteristic.

Unlike with zombies, where the obvious emergency puts me into gear, I always feel like I am swept up into a nice romance movie with these couples. I can start to feel that this couple doesn't need me, that their relationship is more put together than mine.

I am learning to keep focused and snap out of the fairytale.

To the best of their memory, Rita and Steve have not had sex for six years.

As I keep my focus, I ask "What's your hunch about why you haven't had sex for six years?"

Rita is the first one to speak up. "We used to have a pretty good sex life, although it didn't start off all that great. Our honeymoon was disappointing. We only had sex once and we were pretty drunk. We settled in and had a pretty good stretch of sex until the kids came and we got busy."

Steve joins in. "Yah, too crazy busy. I think that one of our problems is that we put everything else besides our relationship first! For me, I don't often feel like having sex because we argue a lot and we both get really angry and mean."

Rita nods in agreement.

Steve continues, "It feels like we are always bickering about something and often that escalates into a vicious merry-go-round. I just am not in the mood when we just had a knock-down-drag-out fight an hour ago."

Rita again agrees. "I also think we lead separate lives."

As if to illustrate what happens frequently to this couple, the nice back-and-forth discussion suddenly bursts into an argument.

The conversation abruptly flares into plain old bickering. Back and forth, who doesn't remember it right, who isn't being treated fairly, who always…(fill in the blank). Bickering shows that each partner feels they don't have power.

The perception that neither partner has power to make a choice, to change their lifestyle, is a canary sign. The canary sign of Person in the Boat sleeping on their River. Adrift. It seems that in the pursuit of being sexual together, they have learned that being sexual gives them less power than not being sexual.

The back-and-forth bickering is something I want to help with right away. It gives me my opening to begin to walk with this couple on their journey.

I discuss the idea that when things go wrong, it is a signal that something is missing. It's time to go where they don't know they don't know—the good part. I know that in order to start up sex, we will need to work to have both Rita and Steve wake up in their Boat Bodies floating on their River Minds. In other words, they must become Responsive to Self.

This can be a long haul. This couple would have already solved their no-sex problem if they could. With couples, I often have to help them build a foundation that they likely never had. The reasons why the foundation isn't there varies, but the outcome is the same. They collaborate very well in maintaining a life together, but to thrive and have sex again, they will both need to wake up.

So, we begin with Intimacy work. It's a great place to start, and I am clear about the path I am leading this couple on.

My little canary is fine and singing a nice song.

It's important to say here that the little canary that I am watching to help me avoid danger is not the sex life of this couple. Not having sex is not the canary. Although it might be a cause for concern, the number of weeks, months, and years it has been since a couple has had sex isn't the most important issue. Not having sex is part of the stories of sex for each partner. The important part is what the story is telling them about their Self.

Bickering and frequent arguing usually means that each person's Self is struggling to feel they have power. The partners are fighting for validation that they are worthy and okay.

At first, Rita and Steve are amazed. After a session where they take time to speak about their experience and their partner is able to hear and witness their experience, they are on a happy high for several weeks.

They make solid improvement. They move away from blaming. They listen to their partner without getting defensive or offended. We start them on the Knee-to-Knee Exercise. They discuss with excitement that they are both showing up in their day-to-day life in a way that they have not done for years.

It's easy to see the first warning sign now, because I now know the missing piece to their couple's story.

The first warning sign was that after an initial couple of times, Rita and Steve did not do the homework. Not just once, which is pretty common. I hate to admit it, but I went for week after week for a pretty long time minimizing the little signs my canary was showing.

I would check, "How did the homework go?" They would look a bit nervous and then either Rita or Steve would have a story about why they didn't do it. Their daughters had a party. They were at their beach house. They were at a conference for their business.

In the meantime, the bickering during session started up again. We would use Process therapy to get them back to their "I Count–You Count" agreement. "I Count–You Count" is a phrase I encourage couples to say out loud to assist in talking and listening in conversation. It means we work to have equal say so. Both stories will be honored.

Sessions continued and they often would lament, "We do so well when we are here in session, but it goes out the window the minute we are home."

Sad to say, I did not even ask about the Knee-to-Knee after a while. A strange lethargy settled over me in sessions. I tried to rouse myself by asking the couple "What's your hunch of why you can't discuss things at home like we do here?"

Several times, I did what couple therapists are trained to do. I said, "I've noticed that the bickering and working together on your life hasn't improved. I've also noticed that you don't do the homework. I'm concerned that our work together is not helpful." Which would be met with, "You are right, we have not applied ourselves and made this a priority. We need to. Let's start our homework again."

I recall a session where we had worked through a disagreement and for some reason Rita had a meltdown and had raged in anger. The session ended without the usual emotional repair.

At our next session I bring up last session. "Last session was pretty intense and I didn't like that we weren't able to end it on a more healing note. I want to ask today what are we working on? What's your goal? I know that I have a goal to help you function as equal partners, but it has occurred to me that that is my goal. I do feel like you need to be able to make emotional connection before we can work on your sex life. But maybe that isn't your goal."

They are silent for a bit, and then each one in turn says, "Yes, we want to learn how to have an emotional trust and bond, and for sure we need that to start up sex again."

I never did get to tell them, "I have nothing more for you. I feel like we should take a break, because progress is waning." No, that's on me. I was adrift, and I certainly missed the little yellow bird on its back, feet in the air.

It is easy to see now, how many stories I didn't really see as stories. They had entertained together and had a great time, they had taken a trip with their kids. They would have these moments of partnering in a life that seemed pretty good except for the no-sex and bickering part. We would reset and begin the whole process again.

The problem was that we began again and again over a course of eighteen months. Somewhere in the process of the third "begin again" I still did not see the cold and still canary lying there. The canary in the mine that could have warned me of the danger.

The canary was my Inner Person Self. Canary down. The thing that was missing was me. The part of me that doesn't just go with the flow of the River, ignoring the Boat and the destination. The part that pays attention and observes the What Is. I had been swept away with this couple's story of their life, not what their experience actually was.

I was in a stupor in my Boat on my River Mind in the sessions with this couple. Though I had pondered why I didn't seem to be helping this couple, how things didn't add up, I was lulled by their charm and that they often seemed to be so happy to be in session. They were on time and regular. We joked that everyone in New York has a therapist, and they had lived in New York. This seemed nice to me. Steve traveled a lot and yet he made it a priority to get a session in the books right after each trip. They often stated how important these sessions were to them.

I did not heed a warning a grad school professor had given to our class of therapists in training. She said, "If a person's effort doesn't match their goals, if you can't seem to make progress—there is always a missing piece. There is something you don't know."

I eventually saw the missing piece. It was the challenging part about Canary Couples having secrets.

I had not paid attention. Then there was an explosion.

Steve emailed and asked for an emergency phone call. This was surprising as he had often insisted that he and Rita always have "together" couples sessions.

He realized he was about to be found out. "Help me," he pleaded on the phone. "Please help me break this to Rita so that it won't be such a blow."

It turned out that when Steve traveled to Europe for his work, he had several girlfriends (he paid for sex) that he would stay with depending on the country he was in. This had been going on for over ten years. He had a separate bank account that was funded by his bonuses. He had developed a closer relationship with one of the women. And he purchased an apartment and paid for her monthly upkeep. This woman was now demanding that he divorce his wife or she was going to out him.

I felt ill to hear this story pour out. I did not see it coming. I only hoped that with my support and work Steve and Rita could repair their life.

I did not see the second explosion coming, either.

It was three weeks before we could schedule a couples session. Nine days after Steve ignited the bomb on my email, I got a call from Rita. She was livid. "We have been seeing you for all these months. Did you know that Steve was paying hookers?"

After the secret broke, we did have one more couples session, but Steve and Rita did not continue couples therapy. It was a sad and unhappy ending.

I am well aware that I am not a perfect therapist. It still hits me hard when I am not able to help a couple. It was my responsibility to stay awake. Painful experiences have renewed my determination to pay attention to whether there is progress or not. I'm more on it when homework exercises are committed to and then brushed aside.

I take comfort from the fact that I am more vigilant now to the progress in our sessions. I am able to talk straight, yet kindly about the lack of effort and will even tell people clear messages like "I don't think I can help you, come back when you feel more engaged in counseling, and let's make sure we are on the same page about what we are doing here."

I bought into this couple being so important and busy that of course they wouldn't be able to easily do the homework. I had succumbed to the idea that they couldn't help but bicker. When all along, Steve needed to bicker; it was how he engaged. I could have helped Rita quit bickering by calling her on her willingness to engage in this way. I could have, but I didn't notice. My canary Self was not acting right, it didn't feel right, but I kept going. I had been breathing the toxic air that had a secret. The missing piece that made the whole River story make sense.

I did not stop to check the "What if?" and so I could not be in the What Is.

150

Jamila Asks What Is

I Count

After a few couples sessions with Tony, Jamila calls to schedule an individual session.

As she sits down for her session, she explains.

"The more Tony shares and the more I think about it, I know I need your help. I have thought about it. I am hurt that my providing a good income for our life is barely acknowledged. At the same time, I do think I am a "workaholic." Work and the fact that I am very good at my job make me feel really good about myself.

"The illustration of the Person asleep in the Boat with the Boat being taken wherever the River takes it, really hit home for me. I do get lost in my thoughts, especially when I am working. I often lose a sense of time."

She continues, "I think it is a fair point that I don't let Tony partner with me. It's not my intent, but I think in my work I am a leader and I am used to interacting from a one-up position. I realize that people will always look to their self-interest and so I am clear I need to take care of myself. I think that is important to do—take care of your own stuff."

As Jamila continues, I note that she is waking up. She is sharing what she is seeing and understanding about the current of her River Mind. She is observing her own story of Self. It is the awake Inner Person Self that is able to see and understand the story of Self. This is what it means when we talk of the painting that has a Boat on a River with a Person in that Boat. "Boat. River. Person." for short.

Jamila is becoming Responsive to Self, waking up in her Boat.

I look at Jamila. "You are doing it right. You are looking at the story you have about your relationship. You are separating yourself from the story. That means you are waking up in your Boat Body on your River Mind. Let's practice."

I ask her, "What is it like to hear Tony say he is hurt that you don't treat him as a partner?"

Jamila pauses. "Well, my first thought is that he is criticizing me. The way he talks, the words he uses are very attacking. Also, I immediately feel angry. He is wrong about this! I partner with him!"

I speak gently as I say, "You are telling me about Tony. I want to know about your experience."

She thinks for a moment. "I just feel confused. Why would he say that? I partner with him."

I check, "What are you experiencing right now as you talk about this? What words describe what you feel right now? Name one or two."

After a pause, she says, "I feel upset and hurt that he would say such a thing about me."

"Upset and hurt are very general. Can you name what kind of upset and what kind of hurt?"

She continues, "I feel like he's saying that I'm not a good partner. It is insulting to me."

"I guess I feel worried I won't be able to make Tony happy. If he's so unhappy, I don't think he loves me. I worry that we won't make it."

She is almost there. I give her an example, "I feel embarrassed that maybe he's right, I have been treating him as if I'm in charge of him."

She repeats her two experiences. "I feel worried. I feel embarrassed."

"There you go," I confirm. "You are starting to describe your experience!"

I notice she is fidgeting in her chair as if to say something. "I don't know how to do this stuff and to talk like this. This doesn't feel like it fits me. I don't talk like this."

I realize it's time to talk about tolerating discomfort. "I understand that it is uncomfortable right now to see this pain you have ignored. If you ignore your What Is, you are ignoring your Inner Self. This is when we grasp and make up stories to get us out of our discomfort. We move away from our truth in order to feel better. It's okay. We all do that. Just know that every time you move away from your pain and discomfort, you go back to sleep."

I offer a suggestion. "Something that may be helpful to you is if you think of it as pushing your Inner Self to focus on the What Is just a little longer than you usually do. Sit in the discomfort, don't back away. Watch the thoughts and how your Body feels while you remain awake to the embarrassment, the worry. Don't jump to a tempting story like, 'I effing partner with him!'"

"Let's notice how easy it is to go back to your story. You often take a path around your What Is (e.g., worry), your experience, to the stories you have about the situation. Don't go to that story. Even if for just a short while. Stay with and focus on the embarrassment, the shame you feel that you are not treating him well and the worry that maybe Tony may not want to stay married."

Jamila is quiet in a good way. She is calm and thoughtful.

I continue. "I want you to go home and tell Tony about your experience when he told you that he doesn't feel like you treat him as a partner."

We discuss the wording that will show her ownership of the experience and her responsibility. Small changes like "I have worry" or "I have embarrassment," rather than "You make me worried."

She practices. "When you tell me that I don't treat you like a partner, I worry that you might be so unhappy that we will divorce. I also feel embarrassed that I have treated you this way."

We continue to discuss how to own her part, her side of the partnership line, and her experience more fully.

She works to say, "I realize that I get angry because I don't want to be a careless, unloving wife. If I respond with a defense, I don't have to think about my experience, my worries, embarrassment, and disappointment. I realize I take the easiest path by making it your issue."

Jamila goes home to tell Tony this.

When Tony hears it, he will get the chance to further practice experiencing his partner and at the same time, remaining clear about his desire to fully partner.

He will be able to practice experiencing her and giving her affirmation without disowning his own desire for the relationship. He can say, "I can see how that is hard!" And at the same time say, "I deserve to be a full partner." I Count–You Count.

Jamila is waking up. She isn't trying to make it go away, she is not blaming Tony, she is awake to her experience and as a result she can experience Tony. It is the beginning of an intimate conversation. I Count–You Count.

We need to separate our experience from those around us. If we don't, we will miss our experience and do a lousy job of experiencing other people.

Our work continues. Practicing being awake in your Boat on your River. Holding onto your experience, so you can look and really see your partner's experience.

Jamila and Tony are on their way to practicing Intimacy.

AWAKENESS

Awakeness
Practicing Integration

Awakeness is the state of being alive.

In this third section, we will discuss how to wake up and practice Awakeness in your Boat Body on your River Mind and how to integrate that into your whole life.

So far in this book we have mostly focused on our Outside Self. Our Outside Self is our understandings and stories about ourselves that come from outside of us. The three Outside Self Stages are Latent, Performance, and Validation.

The Latent Self is about our roles in life and generally where we feel we belong and fit in, or don't belong or fit in.

The Performance Self is about how we feel we are stacking up to our own and others' expectations, how well we do in life.

The Validation Self is about how others show us, validate us that we are okay, desirable, worthy, and lovable.

These Outside Stories of Self aren't the "real story." As long as we listen and tell these stories, we are not very awake.

The "What if?" question helps to wake us, and practicing What Is keeps us awake, alert, and Responsive to our Inside Self. Becoming Responsive to our Inner Person Self is "waking up."

Once we go beyond the Outside stories of self and are awake and Responsive to Self (Inner Person Self), we can access our own wisdom. It is our wisdom and our habits of directing our lives with that wisdom that enable us to Integrate our Inner Person Self into all we do in life.

This section contains six parts representing six areas of practicing Integration in our life.

Part One: Awake Self. We locate our sense of our Inner Person Self by being able to step back from our River Mind and think about the endless stream of thoughts. We also check in and pay attention to our Boat Bodies, noticing sensations, energy, and messages that our Body sends to us. The part of us that is able to observe our thoughts and understand our Body sensations and energy is our Inner Person Self.

Part Two: Awake Anger. Anger is an important emotional experience that can help us discern unfairness. It is often the "gateway emotion" that signals hidden stories of Self and camouflages other emotions. Awaking to anger is important to dissipate its toxic effects on Mind and Body.

Part Three: Awake Partnership. Locating and practicing an awake Inner Person Self is the foundation of a healthy, intimate, and contented relationship. Using the metaphor of a bridge and the abutments that anchor the bridge, we look at Intimacy. "Equal say so" is a phrase we use to describe a functional and functioning relationship. The "I Count–You Count" commitment and dialogue are discussed.

Part Four: Awake Sexuality. Our Sexuality is often both a mirror and the last frontier for our growth, wisdom, and Contentment in our life. Part Four underscores the idea that the highest level of becoming our best self and finding meaning in our life, is to practice fully showing up in all areas of our life including Sexuality.

Part Five: Awake Desire. Many problems about sex come down to arousal for sex and desire for sex. In Part Five, we take a deep dive into how bringing an awake Inner Person Self to your stories of desire, libido, and eroticism can reveal what you don't know you don't know and lead to practicing "Proactive Desire."

Part Six: Awake Sex. In this part we explore what actually happens in sex with the Arousal Pathway, which describes the difference between a Closed sexual experience and an Open sexual experience. And you may have guessed it: we discuss how to have a sexual experience by showing up with your Inner Person Self. Finally, we follow the sex therapy sessions of Erica and Ted through to their graduation and deep sense of Contentment with their sex life.

PART ONE

Awake Self

Life, Only More Awake

Find Your Self

What if the meaning of life is to live the life you have? Not the story of your life, but the What Is life that you are sitting in right this moment.

Finding and lingering in the What Is is harder than it sounds. Although we are given lots of ways to keep sharp and awake during our journey, and to remain present in our life, we don't always wake up or stay awake very long.

There are lots of reasons for this. Maybe when we are present, we are in pain. Maybe we like the story of us and our external self much better than what is playing in our River Mind or the condition of our Boat Body. Yet the things that are keeping us happy may be the very stories that keep us deeply sedated in our life.

And then there is just plain, normal development of our ability to find our Self. In other words, we are human. We start off with the information about our self given to us by the circumstances of our birth, our family, the roles we are in, before we ever think about such things. Our Self of Origin. It our home base self. Which we will always have with us, and are likely to return to again and again. Even if it is to reject the information we started with.

We also compare ourselves with others and try to live up to our story of what we need to do to perform as a human person. We get sucked into this so that we will be desirable to others.

Most of us crave others' feedback, others showing us that we are okay and desirable as humans. We see our self based on external events and feedback from other humans.

Even when we become more in tune and Responsive to our Inside Person Self, it is not a given that we will magically find another human—including if we are married—that is able to respond to their own Inner Person Self so that we can create intimacy and connect the two Inner Selves.

Although it is more likely that we will become more skillful in building an Intimacy Bridge if we are Responsive to our Self and invite Integration into our interactions with others, we more than likely will be tested in our ability to remain awake and Responsive. In fact, the pain and difficulty in our relationships can be our ally in becoming ever more skillful at being present and awake in our day-to-day life.

Yes, we all start with an Outside version of self. Just like in my yoga clsss, where I thought what was happening was an indicator that I was failing, but really, I was doing it right (noticing how my body was responding)—We are doing it right.

And yes, we still have our Inner Person Self that tends toward falling asleep.

The wisdom of Lindy's painting is that the Person in the Boat on the River is not sleeping.

So how do we wake up?

It isn't a one-time "Aha, now we are awake!" It is a practice, a skill. The good news is that you have all you need to wake up in the life you have right now.

You may be very sleepy, but each of us have a wonderful, powerful Inner Person Self. We just need to practice locating him, her, them.

Waking Up

Inner Person Self

How do we go about waking up our Inner Person Self?

First you locate and find your Inner Person Self. The Inner Self is not a story, say of a role you take, or how you perform, or if others approve of you.

Our Inner Person Self is the part of us that asks the "What if?" and the "What is?" to find the What Is. It is the part of us that watches our River—our thoughts and the images that float by in our Mind. Our Inner Person Self tunes into and listens to what our Body is communicating with us via sensations and energy.

You probably noticed that the "What if?" question helps you "Think about your thinking." We are always thinking, and so it may seem like our Mind is our Self—us. But it isn't. Our Rivers pull us along in our Boats all day long and sometimes deep into the night.

Who is it that can watch your thoughts and discern the kind of thoughts you are having? Who can ask "Why am I repeating these thoughts over and over?" "Why is my attention hijacked on this topic?" It is not your Mind asking that kind of question. It is your Inner Person Self that has the power over your Mind. Your Inner Person Self can paddle around in your River Mind. That is, if you are awake and have your eyes open.

This means that you begin to locate and understand your Self by watching the thoughts go by in your mind.

But let's not forget the Boat, our Body.

Did you also notice that "What is?" is a question that needs your body to answer?

The human body is amazing. And wise. We are not awake if we ignore our Boat Body.

Our bodies do not speak to us in words, but in a language of sensation and energy. Our bodies store information, have a memory, and can instantly get messages and memories to our minds in the form of thoughts and images.

Our Body Boats are very wise and skilled at getting us important information. Trouble is, we ignore and detach from our Boat Bodies and get very distressed when our bodies have breakdowns and pain.

Learning to be attentive to our body communicating with us and receive information from our bodies requires us to check in and attend to our Body. We check in by paying attention to the breath, and using all of our senses to gain information about our environment, scanning our bodies for sensations, messages, and energy levels.

Once again, we ask the question "Who is it?" What part of you directs your attention to find out what the Body is telling you?

That part of you that is above the River Mind, that watches the thoughts go by and scans the Boat Body for messages; that part is your wonderful, amazing Inner Person Self.

All of the painting is you!

Contented

The Difference between Happiness and Contentment

The name of my blog on my website is "Contented." Over the years, many people have talked to me about contentment. Most people speak of contentment as if they don't want it. Like it is a bad thing.

> *We have a good relationship and a good life together.*
> *I don't want to be content with a lousy sex life.*
>
> *My partner is passive and seems content with a mediocre sex life.*
>
> *My partner is content to let me do everything.*

And the most anti-contentment (and what sounds exhausting) of all:

> *We never want to be content with our sex life, we want to*
> *always make sure we keep the passion for each other.*

The sentiment that you can't be, never want to be, content in your sex life is expressed every so often when someone will mention to me that they are surprised that a sex therapist would have a blog called "Contented."

There are undoubtedly some differences in what the words "content" or "contentment" mean to different people. But I think that a lot of people use it to mean something they don't want to somehow slip into feeling or experiencing. Contentment is not usually the vision or the goal for a person.

Happiness, on the other hand, is a sought-after commodity. I get lots of happiness talk in my work with couples.

> *I'm not happy with this marriage.*

I just want to be happy.

Life is too short to live so unhappily.

I don't think my partner will ever be happy.

The difference between happiness and contentment is that Contentment is an inside job.

This is why I want to encourage people to practice Contentment with their sex life. The Outside-Self gauge of "Does my sex life make me happy?" is heavily dependent on what others can do for us. Are you able to use my love language? Are you able to arouse me? Do you make me feel desirable and desired?

The practice of Contentment is coming into and resting in the peace you have in your Inner Self. This is a job only we can do for ourselves. We must wake up to do it.

Jamila Locates Self
See the River Mind, Feel the Body Boat

Jamila is back. During her last session. I guided her to pay attention to her confusion and anger, and to use it to wake up in her Boat.

She followed through with the assignment. She told Tony that she was embarrassed and worried about him not being happy.

In their discussion, Jamila realized that she was feeling unloved when Tony complained about being left out. She was worried that Tony wouldn't love her. Although she had not yet shared this with Tony, she brought it in for us to discuss.

I note, "We are needy for people to love us when we don't honor and love ourselves."

Jamila is quick to say, "I don't think loving myself is the problem. Tony and my friends would tell you that I'm too self-focused and 'love' myself too much!"

I say, "It is true that people who only pay attention to their own self-interests seem like they love themselves. But it is the opposite. If you really honor your Inner Self, not the story of self, you have the ability to pay attention to others' interests. When we stay with our What Is when we are talking with others, we are showing that we love ourselves. When we respond and take action based on this higher sense of esteem of Self, rather than a need to have everything lined up to agree with our stories, that is when we honor and love ourselves.

Jamila says, "That's confusing. You are saying that people who always look out for themselves really aren't awake and really don't love themselves?"

"Yes, that is what I am saying. We can test that out by looking at your stories. What are some of the stories you tell yourself about your marriage?"

She replies, "I am a good partner because I earn good money for us to live. I work hard, so I should get to say where the money is spent."

"You have a story that providing financially is a way to be a good partner."

"Yes, I do feel good about that." She nods.

I repeat another possible sentiment: "I'm a smart person because I do my job so well and earn so much money."

I look at her, and she says, "Yes."

"Would it be fair to also say that when Tony comes to you and says, 'I want to spend more time with you, I want to talk more,' that you feel like it is unfair because you have put the time in to be a good partner? Or when he says, 'I want to buy this or get a contractor to do that,' you feel like he is asking for too much? That he isn't realizing what you bring with your job, that he isn't appreciating your good partnership?"

Again, she nods.

"Committed partnerships are good for us because other people don't buy the stories we have about ourselves. So when people question your story, it's an invitation for you to go where you didn't know you didn't know. In this case, you didn't know that your idea of how to be a good partner wasn't holding up with Tony.

"What if there is something you don't know you don't know? What if Tony's experience can tell you something about your stories? Rather than retelling your stories, you pay attention to your What Is. Let's try that.

"Check your thoughts. Are you confused about why he is asking and saying the things he is saying? If you are confused, ask for more information. Don't say, 'How dare you ask!' Don't say, 'I can't believe you are asking this!' Check your Body. What is your body telling you?"

Jamila rolls her shoulders. "I am feeling tense in my shoulders and my head is getting a full and hot sensation. I feel really pissed off."

"Good. Now what do you do next?"

"Well, of course, this feels bad and I do the thing that feels good. I tell Tony off in anger."

"So, in other words, you not only think he's out of his mind for the suggestions, but you are not hearing what he is actually saying his experience is."

We go back and forth and I can see Jamila is beginning to question her story and look both at her What Is and what Tony says is his experience. She is working to wake up.

There are two things to check in order to wake up to the present. Think of it as like the painting we have discussed. To wake up your Person in your Boat, you first need to pay attention to your River Mind. Another way to say it is you think about what you are thinking. What are the thoughts and images you are focusing on?

Secondly, you also want to assess your Boat Body. Our bodies have their own language. If we listen to them, we can benefit from the wisdom. In order to wake up in your painting, you need to check with your Body. What messages is it sending you?

Most of us get overwhelmed if we feel that someone is criticizing us. Why is that? It is because we desperately need to have validation that we are okay. We need validation of our story. Why do we need that validation so badly? We want to feel that we are honorable and worthy and wise and okay. Because we don't believe it for ourselves, we look outside of us for confirmation.

I check in again with Jamila. "What are your thoughts? And what is your Body telling you?"

"I am sad," she says. "My Body feels weighted down and heavy. I think you are right. I get caught up in my story and I don't listen to Tony. It's like I protect myself because I don't want to hear that Tony is unhappy. That might mean that he doesn't love me. I am protecting my story that I deserve admiration and love because I provide for us as a couple.

"Yet I am seeing that I didn't love or respond to myself. I was trying to be okay by performing a role, and by getting my partner to validate that role and that performance. And in the meantime, there was no room for my partner. When he tried to tell me, I got mad and hurt that he didn't validate my story."

I notice that Jamila is not defending herself anymore; she is taking a good look at her shame and anxiety.

She is waking up.

PART TWO

Awake Anger

Awake to Anger
Responsive to Self

Although I discovered that my meltdowns were about anger and grief, I never did make a painting of a meltdown for Lindy.

When I started to write and think about the anger I had carried around for many years, I felt the heaviness that I had been carrying around with me gradually begin to lift. I accepted that I still had anger after all these years, and that I had never honored my anger. I did not protest with a story about the anger. I did not fall back on my excuse of being a counselor. I owned that I still have anger about the leaving the church situation, about my family relationships, and about my marriage. I accepted the human blessing of anger, and as I did, I felt a deep shift within me. Despite all that, I was okay.

With an easing of the shame, came more insight.

Ironically, before I had realized the What Is underneath my story, lots of years ago now, I had made a mixed media piece of art called "Three Blessings." It hangs in my counseling office today. It reads:

> *Three Blessings*
> *Sadness Awakens to reality*
> *Anger Awakens to injustice*
> *Fear Awakens to harm.*

As I began to work through my meltdowns, I thought about the Three Blessings.

In particular, *Anger awakens to injustice.*

I had created the piece after I came across the idea of "clean" anger and "toxic" anger. My meltdowns are an example of toxic anger. The anger was hanging out in my Mind and Body. I could tell myself the story that I wasn't angry, that I was not an angry person. But that was a story, not my What Is.

Meanwhile, I was very sleepy in my Boat and mumbled things like, "I'm over that," "I've done my work," "Hey, it's my family, it's not about how they are but about who I am." Even though I can see now that my toxic anger made me otherwise, I remember saying, "These are the friends and family I have, and I am a loyal and loving person."

The story that had kept me asleep to what my body remembered was a mixture of wanting approval for my decision, fear of being alone, and if I am honest, thinking that if I could just get them to see what I saw, they would come with me. I remember thinking at the time that it seemed that nobody wanted to talk to me about what was happening to me that made me decide to leave my church. Many assured me that they still were my friends, that they still loved me, but no one wanted to discuss my unhappiness or the unfairness of the church culture. I carried a shame that I didn't seem to be all that loving and "Christ-like" as I continued to follow the path out—to leave. My pain and unhappiness with religion still leaks out with criticisms and sarcastic comments about churches to this day. I have more work to do.

I realize that I was working to convince people that I had a right to leave this church because I saw a path to be a more authentic person. I also was hoping some would join me.

But there was a more important Aha, a waking up in my Boat. I remember when I was a kid several someones on several occasions told me that I didn't know what I was talking about. I also have lots of memories of being ignored while I was talking.

Now I wasn't a kid anymore. In fact, it was my responsibility to hear and believe in myself. I had been depending on my role and how well I performed in that role, and the validation I got back as a daughter, sister, friend, wife, mother, and Christian to give me good feelings about myself and define myself. My Outside Self. I had ignored my anger even though it was there to help me out.

We can clean up our toxic anger by facing it, working to see what our anger is showing us. Anger is clean when it wakes us up to our What Is. Clean anger supports our value and lovability and allows us to paddle through the situation. Like "working a problem," we can "work the hurt." We are not the anger, we are able to deal with the anger. It may take some work, but we are not powerless over the problem. We can paddle through the situation. We can work through our sense that something or someone is unfair or unjust and decide and act on what we need to do to advocate for ourselves.

The most important Aha from my meltdowns was that I did not listen to or believe myself. This realization brought a new determination to be Responsive to my Self. I continue to understood more deeply how to wake up in my Boat on my River and how to paddle through my life. Even when I have anger.

Boat. River. Person.

Toxic Anger

Anger Matters

Never expect anyone to take care of your anger. It won't happen. Yet many of us do drop our anger on others' doorsteps like a box of unwanted kittens.

I always want people to realize they have hurt me with their angry outburst and come back and apologize. I hate it and think it is unfair when someone comes back after they have let their anger fly, have thrown a temper tantrum, and they pretend that it never happened. This is like a dog owner walking their dog over to your lawn to do their business. Suddenly they "see a bird" and cross the street to see it better. No bag or shame in sight.

Just as bad is when someone minimizes their angry behavior. "I was just having a bad day." Or the worst, "The way you said that, the way you were talking to me was what caused me to respond like that!"

Those comebacks for anger make me angry. No, that's not right. I feel angry! Better.

Hmmm.

I have anger about how people show their anger. There, that's right.

I am not my anger. I am a Person Self who experiences anger.

I realize that sometimes, I too hope that showing my anger will help a person change their mind, treat me better, or go away.

When someone is angry at me, I realize I tend to do one of two things. I either get super calm and refuse to answer in kind (or at all), or I do a U-turn and become very deferential (ignoring my side of the line) to every nuance of what they need. The term for this is to "fawn." Fawning is a protective response like fight, flight, or freeze. So, when I am in the midst of an angry exchange (we won't call it conversation!), I often protect myself with fawning. Which at times may be the best choice.

There are two things to keep in mind about anger. First, when we ignore or minimize our anger, it does not just fade away. Anger is a wake-up alarm that the body and the mind sound to get the Self's attention. If we hit the snooze button, it will go off again and again. That's the way it protects us.

The second thing I always want to keep in mind is that anger is a blessing, because when we are angry, it is a signal to us that injustice has been done.

It may give you pause to think of anger as a blessing.

Think of it as your Mind and Body alerting you, communicating with you. It is intel, information about your situation.

As I have shared with you, I had determined that anger was a bad thing. In my family of origin, I had witnessed and been the target of painful rage and anger.

I had determined that I would never allow myself to do that. Side note, even though I had made that promise to myself, I had failed on many occasions.

This story that I would not be an angry person—that no matter what, I would remain calm—had done damage to me. It had sedated me heavily in my relationships and how I lived my life. I had hit the snooze button many times. My sleeping through my anger was the cause of my emotional meltdowns and rants. And at times passive-aggressive behavior.

Toxic anger is when you demand that someone else do something. You give them an ultimatum to change something to make you feel better! Or in a case like when I ignored my anger, I demanded of myself that I not be angry. It was like I was striking a bargain to convince people that I was worthy and to stay with me. My "ultimatum" to myself was if you point out the unfairness of the situation, you won't have any friends or family left. This is fear of abandonment.

A problem with toxic anger is, what if the person doesn't do what you want them to do; or they appear to do what you want, only to go back to before when you are not looking. Or, in my case, what if it is to my benefit and protection of myself to be angry? With toxic anger you are dependent on others to keep you from being angry. Meanwhile, you are missing the blessing of your anger.

The reason you rage and make aggressive demands is because you desperately need the person to help you feel better about you. Worthy. Respected.

Anger is a blessing when you attend to the unfairness of the situation by self-soothing the slight or the unfairness yourself. You get yourself back to the knowing that you are deserving of fairness, kindness, love, and respect. You reassure yourself of this fact. Your anger matters; now what are you going to do about it?

You can take care of relieving your anger and have peace again, whether or not the other guy does anything. It is a great relief not to depend on the other person or situation to do anything for you.

If you have anger, treat it like a signal. Woohoo! You are doing it right.

Ignoring the unfairness of a situation creates a poison that dumps into our River Mind.

If we wait for the external world to make us peaceful and happy, then we are at the mercy of others. Our power comes in attending to our What Is.

It is always up to us to take care of our anger.

Clean anger is anger that you notice and honor. You think about what you can do to make the situation okay for you. Since you know it is there to help you, you can work with it to make sure you are aware of what is just and fair. You may need to alert others that you have anger. You may need to speak up and request a fair resolution or an acknowledgment of the problem. Maybe what helps you deal with the anger is an owning and being honest to yourself that you are angry. The best deal of all is not needing anyone to help you feel better and being present to What Is.

PART THREE

Awake Relationships

Bridges and Abutments
Intimacy Bridge

Bridge: *a structure carrying a road or path over an obstacle.*

Abutment: *the elements at the ends of the bridge which provide support for it.*

One of the things I do in work with my clients is talk about an Intimacy Bridge.

To build a bridge you must have two sturdy abutments, two awake and present people that show up like the person in Lindy's painting. Awake Inner Person Self, in a Boat Body, on a River Mind. The whole painting.

An Intimacy Bridge is like it sounds. It means that a "bridge" opens between two people and they are able to get back and forth to each other, to see and understand each other. In the work on a relationship of two committed and partnered people, the building of your side of the bridge is very important.

An Intimacy Bridge is a sturdy two-way conversation that requires that there are two sturdy abutments holding the weight of emotions, experiences, and meanings that may cross back and forth over the bridge. The I Count–You Count Dialog is an example of an Intimacy Bridge.

In our Intimacy Bridge conversation, we take turns focusing on each side of the bridge.

Intimacy is the ability to experience another person while you keep track of your experience on your side of the bridge.

Healthy Partners
Full Partnership

Now that we have talked about the Intimacy Bridge, it's time to talk about how to build your abutment, your side of the bridge.

When couples come to work on their relationship, I tell them my definition of partnership at our very first session.

I define a healthy partnership as when both people have an equal say–equal voice in the relationship.

"Equal Say So" for short.

After putting that definition out there, I step up to my whiteboard and draw the I Count–You Count diagram. I take the time to write exactly the same lists side by side, and then quickly draw a line between them. I have done this many, many times. My thinking is that it adds a bit of dramatic emphasis that helps get people's attention and supports them on what we will be doing next. This is the list I used for Maria and Warren, the Zombified couple:

Mind Thoughts, feelings, emotions, subjective experience(s), needs, wants, desires, preferences, worries, anxieties, fears, your unique problems, issues, challenges, and weaknesses.

Body Energy, needs, sensations, messages/signals, unique conditions and challenges.

It's your job to have this list. Even if you don't literally go up to a whiteboard or make this list on your phone, or get crazy and do something like write it on a piece of paper—this is a basic healthy human skill. To put it in the I Count–You Count language, you are responsible for your side of the line.

Your voice, the real What Is story, comes from your Inner Person Self. In our journey to go from seeing our self from the outside to seeing and understanding our Inner Person Self on the inside, a good place to start is to use this checklist. This will help you check with yourself and become "Responsive" to what is happening inside you.

And having "your say so," your voice, is an abutment, your end of a bridge, that holds your part of a bridge to connect with another person.

In a partnership, your partner needs to attend to their abutment and side of the bridge. It's their job and their privilege to have their own list in their life together.

A healthy partnership is two people making their lists, checking their lists, updating their lists, and talking about their lists at appropriate times. A healthy partnership is two people using their best effort to wake up and deal with the What Is of their list.

After getting my mirror image list up on the board, I turn back to the couple and ask a question. "Why do you think I just wrote the exact same list twice?" The answers vary, and surprisingly very few people connect the equal say so idea to the double list. This allows me to deliver the punch line.

Both sides of the line count! Equally. I Count–You count. This is a picture of a healthy, functioning partnership. In a functioning partnership, each person practices taking care of their side of the line and at the same time they listen, tune in to, and experience their partner's side of the line. Best effort.

Which brings us back to the working definition of Intimacy. The ability to pay attention to and experience another person while paying attention to and holding onto your own experience.

I Count–You Count starts with your Inner Person Self waking up. We wake up by not allowing our River Mind to pull us along, by paying attention to the wisdom of our Boat Body and coming into our What Is of the present moment as often as we can. The practice of Awakeness.

If you are going to attend to your partnership, your first job is to take care of your side of the line. Then you will want to hear about and understand your partner's side of the line.

I Count–You Count.

I Count–You Count.

What Is–What Is

Tony and Jamila are back for a couples session.

Jamila starts. "Tony and I want to work with you on a conversation that did not go well. It's actually something we argue about a lot!"

I look over at Tony to see that he is nodding in agreement.

"Okay." I invite her to begin.

"We had been having a good weekend when on Sunday Tony came to me and said he wanted to talk. I immediately was annoyed, because when Tony asks to talk, he usually has a complaint to make. I was having such a good day and really didn't want to get in an argument."

She continues. "Well sure enough, he wanted to talk about our free time. We usually argue when we try to talk about our social life and vacations."

Tony interjects, "We don't really do anything together. Not like social or fun stuff."

Jamila responds, "Although we do both work a lot, we do stuff together. I am happy with our free time. I think it is important for us to have friendships and a social life as individuals."

This is enough information for me. I realize this couple has had this argument many times before. We don't need to keep going for me to see the painful communication gridlock. We can use what happened this weekend to guide them to begin functioning as full partners. I Count–You Count.

"Okay, let's work on this." I get up and go to my whiteboard. I draw what by now is a familiar illustration to the couple. First a line down the middle. Then I start a list first on one side and then the exact same list on the other side. A check-in list of the Mind and Body.

I review the definition of a healthy partnership. "Happy and Healthy partnerships work to practice 'I Count–You Count.' It's the I Count–You Count Agreement.[8]

"Are you both still committed to the idea that you both count? That you both have equal say so?"

Tony and Jamila nod in agreement.

Okay, remember that intimacy is the ability to experience your partner while holding onto and tracking your own experience."

I sit back in my chair and invite Tony to start.

He begins with "I would like us to find things to do on the weekends and to plan things for our free time. I don't think Jamila really wants to spend time with me. We don't seem to enjoy the same things.

"Speak directly to Jamila," I coach.

Tony turns in his chair to look at Jamila and repeats his point directly to her.

"Jamila, I would like us to figure out how to do more things together on the weekends and when we have free time. I would like us to go on more vacations. I know we don't enjoy a lot of the same things." He pauses.

"And?" I cue him to say the other part.

"I often feel like you don't want to spend time with me."

Jamila looks at me and says, "Yes, this is the same thing he always says. He wants us to plan stuff to do together, to get together with other couples, and most of all, he wants vacations."

I look at Jamila hoping that she isn't done yet. She continues, "We have argued about this so many times and we never get anywhere."

She missed it.

"I can see how it may seem like you can't get anywhere when discussing this," I say. "I wonder, though, if you realize that you didn't really seem to understand Tony's experience, which I believe is the most important part of what he said."

She does not hesitate. "Yes, he tends to want to go on vacation at the most inconvenient times, and the kind of vacations he is proposing tend to be very expensive. I feel like he doesn't appreciate the demands of my work. I can't be taking a lot of vacations right now with the projects I'm working on."

I speak quickly now. "That is about you. That is your side of the line. Although it is important and we will get to what is on your side of the line, right now we are listening to Tony and working to understand what his experience is."

---

8   The I Count–You Count Agreement is outlined in the Appendices.

Jamila tries again. "I feel that the reason we can't talk about this is that…"

I cut her off. "That is about you."

She pauses and looks annoyed, "I guess I don't know the exact words to say. What is it you want me to say?"

I gently review, "Right now, we are working on breaking free of gridlock on this issue. In order to talk about it differently we are using the I Count– You Count Dialog. The idea is to use your equal-say-so partnership to resolve the issue.

"We started with Tony's side of the line. He is talking about his experience with this issue. What did you hear him say his experience of this issue is?"

She is quiet again.

"It's fine to ask him to repeat it if that would help," I continue.

She turns to Tony. "We have argued about how to spend time together and vacation a lot. I do want to spend time with you."

"That's about you," I repeat.

She starts over, "Today I hear you saying that you feel like I don't really want to spend time with you." She pauses again.

"And what else?" I ask.

"It sounds like you are worried we don't really have stuff we like to do together."

I think she has nailed it this time. I check in with Tony. "How did she do?"

"I'm amazed. I have never heard her understand me without getting irritated," he says, sounding very relieved.

Jamila isn't a bad wife for not doing the exercise right. This is what we all do. We aren't curious about what the other person is experiencing because we don't allow for both sides of the line.

In the I Count–You Count Dialog, both sides of the line count.

I look at Jamila. "How are you doing?"

"I'm fine, but this is really hard. I don't think we could do this at home."

I continue, "You are doing really well. You two just broke the gridlock. Are you feeling up to continuing to explore Tony's side of the line?"

She nods yes. "How do I do that?"

"Invite him to say more about his side of the line. You have heard him say his worry that you don't want to spend time with him. That would be a good place to start."

Jamila goes more easily to Tony's side of the line now. "Tony, you said that you don't think I really want to spend time with you. I'd like to understand that better."

He answers, "When I ask you to come along to the store or take a walk, you have often said, 'Not really my thing, that sounds boring.' At first, I would try to convince you that it would be enjoyable just spending time together no matter what we are doing, but it began to be too hard and I quit asking you."

Jamila is listening attentively now. I watch to see if she will keep going. She does. "I am hearing that it has not felt good to you when I answer an invitation by saying, 'No, it's boring.'"

This time I quickly say, "Well done!" to Jamila. She is solidly staying on Tony's side of the line.

We could certainly keep going, but it's important that Tony also get comfortable checking on Jamila's experience.

It's Tony's turn. Tony invites Jamila to talk about her experience of vacations. She shares, "When I think of our vacations, it seems like I always end up feeling bored and somewhat depressed. I don't like most of our vacations. It's always stressful. Starting stressful and stressful when we come back. We always end up being tense with each other."

Tony takes a couple of tries where he gets stuck on defending himself with Jamila being bored. "I try to think of things that you will like." He shakes his head and tries again, "I always ask you when we are planning our vacation." He looks at me.

I say, "Try again."

"Tell me more about feeling bored." He finally is able to truly be on Jamila's side of the line.

Tony has done it. He is now solidly focused on Jamila's side of the line.

We continue on to discuss Jamila's boredom. As she speaks about it, she realizes that what she is calling boredom is more like anxiety, as her thoughts keep being pulled back to work.

The insights start to come quickly for both Tony and Jamila.

As we begin to wrap up our session, I note that instead of arguing if they want to take vacation together, the conversation is now focused on Tony's experience of feeling rejected and Jamila's experience of anxiety. There will be more exploration of both sides of the I Count–You Count Dialog.

Tony and Jamila have accomplished a very good thing.

They each have located their Inner Person Self by exploring their What Is. And through that process they are experiencing each other while not losing track of their own experience.

Gridlock has been broken by a conversation that opened a bridge between the I Count–You Count lists.

Relationships and Self
See Your Inner Person Self

Let's go back to the story of the Boat, River, Person painting. This painting inspires us to keep our eyes open, watch the River, and pay attention to how our Boat is doing.

Yes, we want to be awake. Awakeness is how we live fully. For we only can live in the present moment.

Relationships of all kinds are very much a part of our understanding of our waking-up journey. Our relationships influence our stories and our understanding of ourselves. It is helpful to have different kinds of relationships with different kinds of people and varying amounts of "including your Self." When we live in long-term partnership with another person, the partnership serves as a reminder to keep an eye on our voice, our say so. And, naturally, you will be reminded to tune in to and include your partner's side of the line.

Although relationships give us that opportunity, it is not a given that we will cross over from an Outside Self to an Inner Self. We can get stuck in our stories of who we are and spend our energy on finding happiness and feeling good. Finding a new story instead of finding our Inner Person Self. Remaining adrift wherever our River Mind takes us, as long as it takes us to a place where we don't have pain. It may feel too painful to look at our What Is.

My meltdowns came about because it was too painful for me to feel the full weight of my loss, my anger. Whenever I got close to that pain, I grasped at a story to help ease the dissonance that my body was communicating with me. It wasn't the real story. I was not defective because I broke down with the pain. My problem was that I didn't acknowledge the pain.

So far in this book, we have talked about the way most of us develop our sense of our Self. We have discussed how to hold onto Self and at the same time experience another Self. This is a necessary skill in fully waking up, fully living our life.

Let's revisit the process of how understanding our Self unfolds—the phases of Self Understanding.

The Latent Self. This is Self of Origin. Our birth family and the circumstance we are born into place us in automatic roles with automatic scripts to follow about how to understand who we are. Most of us return from time to time to the safety of our Latent Self, especially when in distress. In this stage our stories of ourselves help us have a sense of belonging, or alternatively cause a sense of never belonging.

The Performance Self. This is our assessment about how we do as a human compared to other humans and compared to our own expectations. We feel good about our self if we feel we do better than others or meet our own expectations. We feel bad about our self if we don't meet our or others' expectations of us. In this stage our stories of ourselves are our anchors, providing directions for decisions.

The Validated Self. This is our understanding of ourselves based on feedback we get from other people and situations of our lives. We actively seek others' positive review of our self. If others validate us, then we feel okay, loved, desired, and worthy. Of course, it follows that if we don't get validation from others, especially others that we are close to, we tend to have stories of not being okay, loved, desired, or worthy.

When it comes to choosing a partner to do life with, it is normal to base that choice on the stories from the Latent, Performance, and especially Validation measurements of self and measure your partner from those same scales.

These views of self are mostly generated from external sources. To put it in the "Boat. River. Person." Language, we are largely asleep in our boats on our rivers.

Yes, we still have the natural wake-up moments of humans. Fight or Flight. Sex. Wake-up opportunities like birth, death, transitions, pleasure, distress, and crises of life. However, most of us hit the snooze buttons of life or fall back into letting our River Mind take our Boat Body along on our thought currents.

Partnering with another person can help us wake up. Specifically, when our relationship isn't working out too well and we are fed up. When our stories of our roles, our performance, and the validation from our partner aren't working to help us feel good about ourselves, it is party time! It is the signal that it is time to go where you don't know you don't know. It's a chance to take note—to wake up.

When we are willing to look at our stories of Latent us, Performance us, and Validation us—all stories about the outside of us, our Outside self—then we can begin to find and understand our What Is.

In this next new phase of understanding Self, we are Responsive to Self. We explore the inner landscape of our Mind and Body to become Responsive to Inner Self. We find out that we have this wonderful wise part of ourselves that we can wake up and start paddling where we want to go. We find that we are okay, desirable, lovable, and worthy. We find this because we finally understand, are awake, and have our eyes open. We understand for ourselves that we are okay, desirable, lovable, and worthy.

We can understand the contrasts of the stories that have guided us and we begin with our What Is. We practice staying awake and living life in the only place we can live life: in the present. The past is not alive. The future is not alive. Any story that we have that gives more energy to the past or the future than the right-now-present is going to sedate us right back to sleep. Because we have located and can be Responsive to Self, we get better at not falling asleep in our Boat on our River.

This is where it gets really interesting for our partnerships and relationships. With a new understanding of our Inner Person Self, we are eager to meet other humans who are awake. We begin to work in all of our relationships to include ourselves. Not the stories of who we are, but our awake Inner Person Self. The Integrated Self is our efforts to live more awake and to invite and understand others' awake Inner Person Selves. It means you are showing up and living in a more alive state.

In a committed partnership, when one person begins to wake up, it challenges the other partner to go to places they didn't know they didn't know. It can get intense. It is not surprising that it's common to run, not walk, back to the safety of Latent stories.

The relationship we have with other people in various states of awakeness and understanding of their Self can be both our biggest challenge and our most valuable, enjoyable blessing in life.

I don't mind repeating this again. It's when our relationship disappoints, goes wrong, and make us feel crappy about who we are that we have the blessing of the Wake-up. Although it doesn't feel like it at the time, it's an opportunity to ask "What if?" and find our What Is.

Include Your Self

Seven Clues That You Don't Really Count in a Relationship

Look at **that** title! It means I get to share a list. I love lists. Here we go!

I sometimes feel regret at how long it took me to discover that I could wake up and paddle. Also, I wish I had learned about the I Count–You Count agreement years ago.

I have my stories I tell myself. I am a good friend to have. I am supportive. I am patient, loyal, and generous. And I love to give great gifts; any excuse will do.

I discovered the meltdowns I was experiencing turned out to come from when I said I wasn't going to be an angry person. That story caused me and my friends quite a lot of pain and suffering.

I have always thought of myself as a solid person that my friends and family could count on. But I discovered that I was working to make the outside of me a good friend—to live up to an idea of what a Christian or a psychotherapist does—but inside I was not awake.

Because I was not awake, I have tended to have many friendships where I was not really a part of the relationship. I realized I always equated love and caring and friendship with giving as much of myself as I could. Looking back, I have often done that enthusiastically, not thinking about the balance. I approached it as "You Count friend. Don't worry about me." That came from my Self of Origin, a story for another time.

It's on me. It's up to us to include ourselves in our relationships. I did not pay attention to my What Is. In regards to friendships I was adrift in my Boat on my River.

I want to share seven ideas of how to check to make sure you are included in relationships and check that you are including others in the relationship as well.

Maybe this will help you include your Self or invite others to include their Self in the relationship much sooner than I did.

One. The B word. There is a song about this word from the children's program *Veggie Tales*. The words come to mind.

> *I'm busy, busy. Dreadfully busy. Much, much*
> *too busy for you, can't you see?*

No one really sings it to others, but whether they realize it or not, frequently telling someone that you are, have been, will be so busy and that's the reason you haven't been in touch is a tell-tale sign that the person you are talking to is not much of a part of your life.

Same goes for people who are frequently late to stuff they do with you because work or life is "so busy."

Honorable mention to the people who say they haven't called you because they "know you are so busy and didn't want to bother you." Huh? Did you just blame me for you not texting?

Two. The other B word. Bored. On this one, I have a bias. I don't think it's cool to be bored. I don't like the word and I admit I tend to look down just a little bit on people who seem restless and bored frequently. That isn't that great of an admission, because it makes me look judgey. So, we will quickly move on from that disclaimer and I will tell you the actual part of the word "bored" that is the point.

If you ask someone to do something, like say go for a walk or another activity, and they say, "Naw, that doesn't really interest me" or "I think that is boring" or some variation of "I don't want to do it"—that is a neon blinking light kind of clue. If spending time together isn't enough all on its own, then you, my friend, are not really including the person in the relationship. I don't care about the stories of this person having the right to do something they enjoy; if someone responds to an invitation in this manner, they have just told you that they don't enjoy you.

They could suggest another activity. I'm just saying.

Three. Not responding in kind—especially with communication. Relationships, interactions, and conversations between humans are commonly imbalanced. One person is more talkative and outgoing. One guy plans ahead and is the one to always get tickets to the game. One person needs extra support for a hard stretch they are going through. Your person who cuts your hair talks freely about her personal life or is skillful at asking questions to get you over-talking about your life.

I am not saying everything has to be fifty-fifty, always exact. My advice on this is that you pay attention to whether you are always the one putting yourself out there in the form of sharing emotions, using energy and effort, spending money, and gifting. If you are doing more than the other person, it is a clue.

Depending on the relationship, you can talk to them about it. With a good friend or family member, I encourage you to talk about it with them.

If you are giving in a supportive, generous way that is imbalanced, it is helpful to say, "I may not always be able to do this, but I want to do this to support you now." Next time, if things haven't changed, when you find yourself wanting to give in a big way, maybe just sit on your hands.

Another option is to moderate, cut back in the giving department to more closely match the level of effort of the other person.

Although I am old enough to remember when people kept in touch with phone calls, it really is more the texting and Facebook situation now. Texting is not really that great if it is the main way you communicate. Some couples have a blistering fight, profanity included, by text. It's always curious to me to think of having a text fight while you are at work and coming home to dinner. How does that work?

But my main beef with texting is when I share an emotion or something about life, or make a bid for connection, and the response is too short, or doesn't match the communication. The brevity of texting seems to be used as an excuse to keep it short, and detached as in "I don't need to go there."

Here's an example of a response I got after asking a friend to get a coffee together in October.

Friend: Hello. Let's plan on getting together after the New Year. My house is going to be full through the holidays with my family. I'm blessed! I'm hosting, and I'm very busy. [Crossed eyed emoji.] How are you?

Me: Sounds like you will be making some nice food and memories. Enjoy! I am sad and dragging since the time change. A bright spot is that we will be spending a few days with my son and my aunt and uncle at Christmas. Otherwise, I will rest and get to lots of yoga classes.

Friend: I hope you have a Happy Thanksgiving! [Three turkey emojis.]

Those turkeys are festive, but feel empty. It's October and my friend is not available until January? We have missed each other. Yet, I think that in today's world, the exchange of texts may qualify as friendship?

True story, I have at times sent longer texts to update someone on a situation or something I am going through and have gotten a one-letter reply: "K." Our relationship is so imbalanced that this person can't be bothered to type the "O."

Okay, that's a LOL! Kinda. To me it speaks to doing the least amount of work possible because the communication with me isn't that important.

But more than that, if we are going to use text in our relationship, you need to use text in the relationship. Respond to what I have shared. Otherwise, it is the equivalent of looking at someone and saying nothing. Crickets.

I now more readily pay attention when I share details of my life and the other person doesn't. Whether in person or on text.

Four. Not asking questions. People who don't ask questions about you don't really include you in their life. The conversation is only about stuff they are interested in. You ask them questions, and they will answer at length. Yet they don't show any interest in your thoughts or your experience or your life. Just in case you don't know what I mean here, although they may like the idea of you, they likely are not that interested in you.

Five. Not tracking others' lives. Facebook has challenged me with this one. Many years ago, I decided that I didn't like myself and my judgey-ness when I would be going through Facebook. So, I quit Facebook. I have not regretted it.

However, I am still surprised when someone assumes that I know information like invitations to parties or so-and-so is pregnant, or assumes that I have been tracking their life on Facebook. It is interesting to me that people don't notice that I am not on Facebook. Quite a few have forgotten that I have shared—numerous times—that I am not on Facebook. That means that for sure they don't remember me sharing my heartfelt experience about deciding to go against the flow of the crowd and remove myself from Facebook altogether.

But even if I think about non-Facebook conversations, I notice there are very few people who track our conversations and my life events well. I also notice I have to use care and effort to track others in my own life.

I notice how disappointing it is to think I am included in someone's life, only to have to update them yet again. This feels like they aren't that interested in me and my life. These kinds of relationships are tiring. When I stop to think about it, it is not really me being included in the relationship and so I should conserve my efforts.

Six. Time spent together. I know that I am not much a part of a relationship when there is a cavalier detachment about time spent together. No preparation of thought given to how to spend time enjoyably together. Just take it or leave it. If there is time, fine. If not, fine.

To me this shows up as a lack of initiative unless there is a convenience for the person. For example, birthdays. Another reason I dislike Facebook is that I still get birthday wishes from people I haven't talked to in years. I think that comes from my old Facebook account, or it's still in their online calendar. It doesn't seem that sincere if the only time I hear from you is on my birthday. Happy Birthday doesn't really go that far for me. If you spend time with me, then birthday wishes go much further even if we don't do anything special.

Going out to eat sometimes feels this way to me as well. Especially if that is the main way we spend time together.

Seven. No emotions, feelings, or subjective experiences. Conversations about persons, places, events, or things can only be interesting for so long. Not talking about how you feel or the experience(s) you are having and not answering questions about feelings, emotions, and how you experience life is a holding back in the relationship.

Likewise, not asking me about my feelings, emotions, and how I experience life is a sign to me of limited engagement, that I am not really included in this relationship.

Many people may know this stuff already. I only began to learn this as I began to work with couples. It's where the I Count–You Count work started.

The Promise

Attend to Your Side of the Line

In the last chapter, I gave some clues to look for to be clear about some situations where you are not really included. In addition, I suggest that you make a promise to yourself to know what is "on your side of the line," be Responsive to your What Is, and practice Awakeness.

The I Count–You Count agreement will help you locate your Inner Person Self and practice including you in your relationships. It is very powerful to make a commitment to your Inner Person Self that you will keep this agreement for two reasons: to honor your side of the line and to honor other people's side of the line.

The I Count–You Count Agreement

When I draw the I Count–You Count graph on the whiteboard, it is two identical lists of different aspects of a person's experience including both the River Mind (thoughts, feelings, needs, wants, fears, and weaknesses) and the Boat Body (sensations, energy, and messages). In between these two lists is a line. When I refer to "your side of the line," it means your particular list.

The I Count–You Count agreement has ten points.

- Your side of the line is your privilege and responsibility. Tend to it well. Be loyal to it. Advocate for your Self—your side of the line.
- You Count. It's your job to make sure you count in a relationship. Especially if you are interacting with someone who does not act like they agree that "You Count."
- You don't Count more than anyone else and you don't count less than anyone else.
- Healthy relationships follow the I Count–You Count agreement always.

- If any person does not care about your side of the line, they are toxic to you. As with everything that is toxic, you need to limit and protect yourself from exposure.
- If someone authentically works to know and understand your side of the line (even if they have been toxic before), take them up on it, and reciprocate as soon as possible.
- Make sure you truly understand your partner's experience, whether you agree with it and think it is right or sane, or not. If someone says something, believe them. (The exception is if you find someone is telling a lie, the way to point this out is from your feelings/emotions on your side of the line. "I feel confused because what I experienced is…." Hold onto your What Is, it is helpful whether the person is truthful or not. When someone isn't being real with you, it's your job to advocate for yourself. Even if that means avoiding or ending the conversation.)
- If it becomes apparent that someone is not at all interested in your side of the line, don't continue to tell them about it. Begin to describe your experience as "I don't feel understood" or "I don't feel heard." Choose carefully whether you tell someone this out loud or you clearly state this to yourself in your mind.
- If you are in an argument that is gridlocked (you keep coming back to the same painful place), break the gridlock by asking the person about their side of the line. Get it clear. Understand the other person's side. Validate what you know about their side of the line. Make sure they tell you about their side of the line, their experience—not your behavior or what they want you to do.
- Once you have very solidly delved into their experience, ask them if they are ready to hear about your side of the line.

One last thing. Keep an eye out for the sneaky reasons either you or another person moves into the "I Count more because" stance. Things like I Count more because: I earn more money, I'm smarter than you, I'm more likable than you, I'm better looking, or I have more power than you (networks, support of people, luck, money).

Working through the I Count–You Count agreement may take some time for both of you to be very clear about your sides of the line. The next step is to ask "How do we move on from here?" and "How do we make sure that both sides of the line count?" Most of us will be tested to hold onto our side of the line until our partner is willing and able to practice the agreement that both sides of the line Count. I Count–You Count. Don't forget your promise to yourself, that no matter what, I—my What Is—counts.

PART FOUR

Sexuality

Are You Happy?

Stories of Sex

Are you happy with your sex life? Are you happy with how you do sex?

I doubt many of us would say an enthusiastic "Yes!" Most of us would have at least a little stab of anxiety, a worry that the question is a trick question.

Perhaps there is something out there that we don't know about, or something we don't realize we are doing or not doing. Are we keeping ourselves attractive enough? Are we up on the new and exciting? What is it that other people do to have so much sex? Did my partner somehow get you to ask this question? If we answer the question, will people know our secret?

The reason this seems like a trick question is because it is.

If we think of Shatima, the young lady who came to therapy to learn how to do sex, we begin to see why the question isn't helpful. When it comes to sex, we are not awake. We wait around for sex to wake us up.

We ride the River of our life, keeping a look out for sex to thrill and reassure us that we are okay in the sex department, and that we are alive. We wait for the spontaneous sexual arousal to wake us up. And it often does, or doesn't.

It seems to me that we pursue the wake-up of sex more than the experience of sex. Don't believe me? Let's look at the stories we have about sex. What is it that gives you that discomfort about sex? From my sex therapy work, I see that most of the time it has to do with anxiety or trouble in getting to the wake-up of sex. Arousal.

What if you didn't wait for sex to wake you up, but you were awake as you entered into an arousal wake-up and sexual experience?

Shatima was working really hard to find the path to good sex. She was looking everywhere she could think of to solve this problem of not feeling good about her sex life. Everywhere except inside herself, her inner world, her painting.

So now, after you have checked in with whether you feel good about sex or not, let's move to "What if?" What if you could enter sex awake instead of waiting for the wake-up to come along? What if you could access and initiate your sexual desire from your Inner Person Self? What if you could paddle your Boat wherever you wanted to go?

What if you stayed awake during sex?

If you stopped at that sentence and re-read it, raise your hand.

I hear someone somewhere saying, "What are you talking about? I'm awake. I love sex. I certainly am not sleeping during sex!"

That is exactly what Nick said to me in a session. Nick and his wife, Chloe are a Zombified couple. Zombified couples are all about the sexual wake-up and very little about the being awake. It was clear to me from the first session that Nick's story of himself, that he is "very sexual," is what he follows in his sexual activity. He is a poster child example of seeking the wake-up moment.

The distress that he and Chloe have is because they fight about when and how they start to have sex. Specifically, what Chloe does to start sex. How sincere she is, how spontaneous she is (shows she really desires him), and how often she initiates. In other words, Nick is wanting Chloe to wake him up, get him aroused for sex.

Nick's protest gives me the opening to take the couple through the process to find the real experience, instead of Nick's "highly sexual" story.

We explore the "What is?" of how it really is for this couple when they are having sex. A familiar not-awake story comes to life.

Though they have worked out how to get aroused, Nick is always reminding Chloe that she needs to do that like she really, really wants sex. After he is aroused, he quickly zones out. It's as if he dives into the River of his Mind and does not surface until he has an orgasm. He doesn't really see or hear Chloe, and she knows it.

And she doesn't really care. Although she would never tell Nick this, she is in her own River. During sex she hangs out thinking about things that are way more interesting than what Nick is doing. "It will be over soon," and she won't have to worry about sex for a day or two. Nick will be in a good mood and task completed.

Nick's story is that his needs are to feel sexual desire from his partner, and at a certain frequency. Chloe's story is that Nick needs this and it's best just to get it over with.

Let's look at the story under this story. What is Nick's story telling him about his Self? He doesn't feel good unless his partner's actions show him he is desired. He has sexualized his understanding of his Self. As he pursues feeling good about life in this manner, his Inner Person Self is asleep. He has no idea how to paddle to a Contented sex life or be present during sex.

Although you don't have to be a zombie to "sleep" through sex, any story about sex that is dependent on others to make you happy isn't the best story.

The most helpful story is always about what is happening with your Inner Person Self. Are you awake in your Boat on your River? When you are awake about sex and during sex, you no longer will have this worry about sex or your need for your partner to help you be happy in sex.

What if the best part of sex wasn't really about the wake-up? Although it's pretty nice. What if it feels wonderful to listen and connect with your body and your partner's body? What if sex is an entering into attunement and clarity of who you are? What if you are so awake during sex that you feel that every part of you is fully present? What if you feel attuned, dialed in with your partner, and you feel fully awake and fully alive? And with that aliveness, a sense of love for yourself and your Body and your existence?

Communion with your Body. Listening deeply to what your Body is communicating directly to you, the Inner Person Self in the Boat. What if the attunement of your Mind, Body, and Self helps you feel alive, at peace, worthy, whole, and joyful.

That is a lot of "What ifs." We haven't even started on the What if you were able to have that experience with another person? Each "What if?" invites you to the What Is of your Self and Sex.

Check the story. If any story promises happiness that is dependent on anything outside of your Inner Self, it is only a story that will keep you happy as long as everything outside you supports the story.

Are you happy with your sexual experiences? Are you happy with how your partner starts sex, has sex with you?

Our Sexuality is the stories we have about sex and what those stories tell us about Self.

"Are you happy?" is the wrong question.

He/Him/Their/They

Responsive to Self in Your Sexuality

I know first-hand how uncomfortable and sometimes unpleasant it can be going to places you don't know you don't know.

In the mid-2000s, I was able to put the letters CST and CS right there after my name. CST stands for certified sex therapist, and CS means certified sexologist. I had many Aha moments in my training and the Aha's keep coming to this day.

Pronouncing the word "impotence" just like it reads on paper, (using the sound "po" rather than the "puh" sound) to a urologist. Who was my client. Who wasn't impressed. Who corrected the pronunciation to "impuhtance." Embarrassing.

The conversation with a client who used the phrase "down low" and I thought he meant keeping a secret. Instead, although it was indeed a secret from his wife, it meant he was a part of a group of men from his church who were having sex with each other. Gosh, that was messy.

Tangles with colleagues about sex positive versus sex negative, sex toys, homosexual templates, and peer-to-peer supervision. Exhausting.

In retrospect, I know when I started my training the appeal of sex therapy for me was a very narrow and naïve focus at first. I really liked the idea that sex could be very emotionally, mentally, and physically intimate. I was drawn to the elegance of Intimacy, and started talking about it by using the phrase "3D sex." I still talk about that to this day, and I still feel drawn to anything and everything that demonstrates two human beings fully experiencing each other.

One particular Aha and chaotic moment that did not feel good was when I met Tommy. I met him at a sex therapy training. This was still in my narrow excitement to "help happily married monogamous couples have better sex" days. At that time, I didn't realize how white and middle class that was. I had not begun yet to take into account what the word "Sexuality" could mean.

At the beginning of our class, we all went around and introduced ourselves. I noticed Tommy had short, short hair—a striking haircut. Tommy was wearing a baggy T-shirt and Levi's and beige work boots. The thing was that between the voice and soft, smooth face, I saw and unconsciously registered Tommy as a woman who was dressed casually. It seemed like she liked hiking or maybe sitting around a campfire.

Later during a class discussion, Tommy made a point and it inspired me to make a point. In what felt like a polite manner, I said, "She makes a great point and I would like to add…" to which Tommy immediately interjected and said, "HE!" very loudly and firmly. Tommy corrected my assumption of his gender.

I had a story of gender that I had never given a thought to. Nothing in my upbringing or professional training had ever questioned that story.

My River Mind pulled my Boat into rough water that rocked me back and forth, and I felt the back of my neck tighten.

I continued my point, but inside I was shaking. It took me quite a while to calm down. "How was I supposed to know that she identified as male?" "She, he certainly doesn't seem male to me!" "Can you even do that?" "Decide you want to be a man?" Mind blown. Messy. Painful. Messy.

That was a lot of years ago. I wish I could report that Tommy advocating for the pronoun that fit him helped me understand. It did get the ball rolling, but I had my own journey to understanding my own story of sex and what that story was telling me about my Self.

That day I still did not know what I didn't know about Sexuality and Queer Theory. I didn't know or imagine why someone would embrace being a transexual, or why calling yourself asexual, gray sexual, or nonbinary was so important. I didn't know about much other than my own narrow understanding of sex and relationships.

Yet that day Tommy introduced me to one of the most important lessons of my life. Although I did not yet know that Sexuality is not just a neat and tidy "yes or no" or narrowly defined to whatever culture or context a person happened to be born into, I will never forget how Tommy stood up for how he wished to be addressed. He was awake and Responsive in his Boat on his River Mind. His sexuality honored and backed up his awake Self.

Since then, many other Tommy situations have entered my life. Each is a teacher. Tommy was further along on his Sexuality journey than I was. He was Awake and Responsive to his Inner Person Self.

Yes or No, Either Or
One Hand

In the early 1990s I was working on my graduate degree in counseling at a Christian University in the Midwest. I have often thought of one particular class and the discussion that the professor led. We were studying theories of counseling and philosophy. A good thing for new psychotherapists.

Near the end of class, the professor asked each of us to share which counseling and philosophy resonated the most with us.

There were a lot of "Holistic Christians."

Quite a few said, "Cognitive Christians."

Two just said, "Christians."

A "Behavioral Christian."

Lots of "Christian," as to be expected at a Christian university.

As I listened to each fellow student, I noticed no one said Psychodynamic or Humanist. I rethought my answer for just a second, but decided I was really clear and to go with the authentic answer.

I was next to last to answer. I said, "Humanistic Christian!" Like a live studio audience, the class immediately erupted into laughter. There was a short pause after the laughter, and the student to my left said, "Holistic Christian."

It was the end of class. The professor said, "Good! You all have some ideas for your counseling foundation. It will serve you well." We were dismissed.

Even at that time, I knew the laughter was because they thought I didn't understand what I said. They didn't think these two could go together. You couldn't follow the teachings of Christ and make your own inquiries and create your own meanings. No, to the class, you couldn't really be a Christian and a Humanist at the same time.

However, at that time, I **was** working on being both a Christian and Humanist at the same time.

Though a bit embarrassed that my classmates thought that I didn't understand, I was more frustrated that no one else seemed to see how these two actually did go together. No one came up after class and said, "Hey, what did you mean?" Their laughter was an indication that they had automatically responded with a "No, that is not Christian!" They were in the "yes or no" thinking of "What is a Christian?"

Though I couldn't have said it at the time, in regards to my Christian faith, I was on a path to becoming more of a "yes and" and a "both and" thinker.

I was able to hold out both of my hands. I did not choose one hand and reject the other. I was using "Two-Handed Thinking." This idea that one thing does not automatically disqualify another comes from Eastern cultures.

Here in the "West," which is the United States for me, most of us use "One-Handed Thinking." This is thinking or making decisions based on yes, no, either, or. We work to decide which hand and go with it. Eastern cultures are more apt to work to answers and solutions that use both hands, that include both the realities represented by both hands.

For example, you can feel well even though you have a chronic illness. You can have an overall feeling of Contentment even though a part of your life is a struggle and a grind. You can feel wealthy even though your bank account is low. You can love someone and at the same time have a painful anger about something they did.

These are pretty everyday examples. When it comes to our stories of sex and what those stories tell us about our Inner Person Self, most of us get "yes or no-y."

Sexy or not sexy?

Sexual chemistry or no sexual chemistry?

Real man or not a real man?

Needs met or needs not met?

Desirable or not?

Yes or no? Stories about things outside of us, telling us about us. Allowing our Inner Person Self to sleep.

I invite you to wake up to What Is in your hands and consider that your What Is may include both.

Queer: Uncommon, Not Normal, Not Straight

Asexual

Although I am a sex therapist, I can't keep up with all the sexualities, genders, activities, and things people are aroused by. I am okay with that.

It wasn't always so. At least I didn't realize it. Earlier I shared that my reason for even studying about sex was very, very binary. Yes or no. Christian, white, middle class.

My journey has been weird. Writing this book became a constant journey into what I didn't know I didn't know. Some time ago I began to hear about this thing called Queer Theory.

One thing that Queer Theory pointed out to me is to not go with "yes or no, either or" thinking. Go with "both and." Look what is in both of your hands.[9]

An online search of a definition of Queer Theory will read something like "A way of thinking that dismantles traditional assumptions about gender and sexual identities." Queer theory challenges the idea that normal or standard sexuality or gender is the correct way and that anything that does not appear standard or normal is wrong or deviant.

Another definition: The validation, empathy, and witness to differences in sexuality and gender from the norms of and within social systems, practices, and ideologies.

How can you do that? If it doesn't make sense to you, how can you be okay with something that is "not normal"? The best way is to not let whatever it is pull you along while you "sleep."

I say that if you wake up in your own Boat, you won't need to be stressed or need to do anything about others. You just paddle your own Boat.

---

9   "Yes or no" is a "binary" outlook. "Both and" is a "non-binary" outlook.

When we are introduced to something that seems foreign to us, it is likely to be uncomfortable. We may take shortcuts to waking up in order to deal with our discomfort.

I love my partner, but I am not in love.

I need _____ to be happy.

I am broken.

I'm not sexual.

I can't give my partner what they want.

To me, it doesn't matter so much if you are hetero, homo, transsexual, transgender, LGBTQIA2S+[10], BIPOC[11], and/or some new acronym that is probably already out there—it matters if you are awake in your life.

To be clear, giving yourself a label is important to honor who you are. And the realities in that title, label, description are important. Yet I am most interested in your What Is for you as a human being. The story of your Inner Person Self. I want to see if you have discovered that you can wake up yet.

Even as wonderful as it may seem to find and locate your What Is and a way of describing your What Is, I am hoping you will go beyond seeing yourself as belonging or not, comparing yourself to expectations wherever they come from, and seeking validation from outside sources. My wish for you is that you become Responsive to your Inner Person Self. I am hoping that you see the whole painting, that you are an awake Person Self in your Boat Body on your River Mind.

Whatever you think about sex, your story of sex, it's what that story is telling you about your Self that I am most interested in.

So, for example, if you tell me you are transexual, I want to know if you are using your whole painting. Are you awake in your Boat on your River? Or are you doing things to belong, perform, and feel desirable?

If you have decided to live your life as a person of the opposite sex than you were born with, or as a non-binary person, I want to know if you are awake with that. At peace? Content?

My mission is to help people in their relationships and sex lives by helping them wake up and move out of passivity into Responsive, Integrated, and Contented lives.

---

10 LGBTQIA2S+ is an acronym for Lesbian, Gay, Bisexual, Transgender, Queer and/or Questioning, Intersex, Asexual, Two-Spirit, and the countless affirmative ways in which people choose to self-identify.

11 BIPOC is an acronym for Black, Indigenous, or People of Color.

All of this talk about waking up applies to a new What Is that is turning up more frequently in my office. Asexuality. It is a sexual orientation. The word means someone who does not experience sexual attraction, or experiences very little sexual attraction, or little or no sexual attractions, and also—very important—they are good with that. It does not cause them distress, but rather relief and or peace.

The meaning of Asexuality will vary from person to person, so thinking in terms of a continuum can be helpful. For example, one side of the continuum might be a person who experiences sexual attraction yet still identifies as Asexual. On the other side of our Asexual continuum might be a person who does not experience sexual attraction or have an interest in sex at all. There are numerous varieties along that continuum. For example, someone who only experiences sexual attraction after a strong emotional bond has formed (demisexual).

Asexuality is just one of many stories of sex that people have, but it serves as an example that whatever your story is, the most important part is that you are awake and mindful of what that story tells you about you.

If your story is that things that are purple turn you on, give you sexual energy, make you sexually excited, then my question for you is "Are you awake?" Does your attraction to purple come from your Self or is it the story of Self? A story of Self would be to say without too much thought, "Everyone knows purple is the color that turns people on," while ignoring if you really do like it. Do you just want to be sexy and excited so you go for the purple? Or is it when you see purple you feel content, relaxed, luxuriant, excited, and ready to have sex.

If you have the value and belief that sex is only for marriage, then I would ask is it the passive sleepiness of someone who must play the role of a good Christian, must perform as a Christian to be affirmed as a Christian? Or on the other hand, is it because you want sex to be with someone who you are committed to and you wish to build Intimacy before jumping too quickly into sex with someone? The first way has set many people up. When push comes to shove, they may end up on the "bad Christian" list—at least in their minds. The second way has its detractors who feel it is too narrow a way to look at sex. They would say sex doesn't need to equal love.

I find it helpful to handle the many diverse beliefs and ideas about sexuality by using the standard of Contentment. Each individual must paddle their own Boat on their River Mind. My job is to help people be awake to paddle to where they really want to go, and to remind them about Contentment.

The following story about Janet illustrates how important it is to be awake to What Is.

Janet had been dating Edward for eight years. Recently, Edward had been talking about marriage. Janet and Edward had argued about marriage a lot. She had come to get some clarity for herself.

She begins.

"Edward is a good guy. We have a lot of fun together. I'm just not sure I'm right for him, and I'm definitely not ready to get married."

I look down at my notes. "You've been dating for eight years?"

She nods and continues. "I know that's a long time, yet neither of us have the jobs we went to school for. I have a student loan and I'm still living with my parents." We spend time talking about the job she really wants.

Then she says, "It's a bummer that I have not found a job in earth sciences. I knew my degree would make it challenging to find a job, but the reason I came to you is more stressful than not finding my dream job."

I remain quiet as she wipes tears from her eyes.

"I think I am Asexual."

I give a soft "Hmm" to let her know I am listening.

"I've been reading about this. Edward and I have such different ideas about sex. He says he needs me. That all he thinks about is being with me. That's why he wants to get married."

She continues, "I am not so sure about what he says. First of all, I just don't understand why sex is so important to him. It seems like all of our dates have to end in sex or he is unhappy.

"Early on, we used to try all kinds of things with sex. Since we are Christians, we still haven't gone all the way."

I ask what "all the way" is.

She answers, "Intercourse, penetration.

"Lately, I have come to dread sex with him. He used to always try to touch me and get me aroused, but I told him 'no' so many times that he doesn't try anymore. So now, I just give him hand jobs. It's getting more difficult to do that. I do want to be a good partner, but I hate doing this. I don't want to even think about sex. I love Edward very much, but I don't want to marry him and I am not at all interested in sex. That's why I think I might be Asexual. I feel bad for Edward."

I already have doubts that Janet is Asexual, but it will be for her to make that call. My best way to help her is to help her wake up in her Boat.

As Janet and I work together, we will start with some "What ifs" What if you listen to yourself that the way you are having sex isn't good for you? What if you might enjoy another way of physical contact more? Would you like just holding each other? What can you do during a sexual experience that supports your Self, honors your Self, your thoughts, needs, wants, and desires?

Any story that diminishes or ignores Self and keeps us sleeping in our Boat is not a good story for us.

Our sexuality is just one of the ways we have a relationship with our Self.

The meaning of life is to live your life to the fullest. Your life. Your Awake Self life.

Asexuality that says that Self is worthy and important, and is equal and needs to be included in relationships, is trustworthy.

Asexuality that ignores what you know, your feelings and desires, is very unreliable.

So, it comes down to your relationship with Self.

Janet's relationship with Self is Latent. She is playing the role of a sexual partner in order to be in a relationship with Edward.

Our work together is to move her to where she listens to her Inner Person Self, and wakes up to her What Is. Then she will know where to paddle her Boat.

As we continue our work together, she moves past her attachment to Edward as a friend and companion to realize that he isn't as much fun as her stories have been telling her. She realizes that "sex" is the main activity they do together, and Edward seems increasingly bored if sex isn't on the table.

She reports back that she realizes her River Mind has told her the story that she needed to have the sex-focused relationship in order to have a boyfriend. She is determined to talk with Edward to discuss more activities.

After several talks with Edward where he isn't able to listen to her side of the line, and mocks and puts down her experience, she makes the decision to break up with him. She expresses worries that she will be lonely and perhaps never find a partner, but this isn't working for her.

Janet has not yet returned to tell me if she is Asexual or not, but I know she has started to wake up.

Is Porn Bad?

It's a River Thing

There is one question in sex therapy I really don't like to ask.

Sometimes I get tricked into asking it, when a partner pulls the topic out to discuss it.

Though I don't like to ask about it, I do. If I can, I try to ask it once my clients have had an Aha or two, once they are waking up in their Boat on their River. For sure I ask it when it is obvious it is part of the problem (whether they are awake or not).

The question sometimes arrives before I or my clients are ready.

When I do ask it, I have to be ready. In leading my clients on their journey to what they don't know they don't know, I need to be ready to cross this treacherous topic. The crossing can be exhausting, and not everyone makes it. With the right tools, such as the wisdom of the painting, it is much easier.

Fantasy

Before I ask someone the "hot potato" question, it is often helpful to discuss fantasy. Fantasy happens in our Minds. Fantasy is a movie that plays in your Mind that your Body likes and responds to. The ability to imagine and create different stories in our Minds is one of the pleasures of life. Fantasy, stories we have in our Minds, are actually pretty fascinating. We can create any kind of story.

And there are so many, many stories—especially about sex and Sexuality. We live in a global world. You may live on some island far into the ocean, and yet you will be able to know just about anything that happens on earth. Sex and Sexuality have become not only global, where sex customs and cultural imprints have fused into infinity and beyond, but now sex activity is like a random-number generator. At any time, anyone or anything could be used for sex or as a part of a person's understanding of themselves.

Sex has grown into a huge and unpredictable thing. Where once we were told to find our fantasies to rock up our sex life, we now can have an infinite number of fantasies with one swipe on our phone.

Fantasies come in all shapes and forms. Little stories and big stories. We tell ourselves stories to lift our mood, give us something to focus on besides the "feel bads" of our life, or give us the story to feel worthy and desirable. Food, scrolling our phones, becoming wealthy, writing a book, getting skinny, hot sex, sexy cars, traveling, designer homes, designer clothes, early retirement, becoming a famous musician, YouTube, TikTok, TV, and porn. I could keep going.

Fantasy offers a sense of new energy, feels good, and rewards us with dopamine just by focusing on the story presented. Think of when you have a vacation scheduled, some time off. Most of us have a story of how we are going to enjoy the vacation. We may run through it every day before the vacation because the story is very enjoyable. The fantasy, the story of how we hope to have a vacation, is very enjoyable in the days leading up to the vacation. I'm sure that for many of us, when we actually arrive at vacation and it looks nothing like the story we had told ourselves, we are disappointed.

The thing that fantasy does is it offers a "What if?" solution to help us feel better. Not all "What ifs" take you to What Is.

In sex and Sexuality, fantasy is a way for us to ignite sexual arousal, communicate to a partner, and tap into deep truths about ourselves—even the fantasies that do not serve us.

An example of a fantasy that may not work out well is when we get caught up in limerence. *Limerence* is the official name for a story that we begin to tell ourselves about another person. The story feels good. It promises that with this other person, we will be happy, we will be fulfilled sexually and/or emotionally.

We can see ourselves being happy so well that our brains actually secrete chemicals that give us a feeling of euphoria when we go back over the story. The pull and current of the River Mind is strong. The story promises us an end to our sadness, depression, or feelings of worthlessness. It is so compelling and intense that we begin to feel as if (act as if) the story is real. Depending on if the person we have limerence for likes the story, we may have a mutual limerence (love story, infidelity, affair) or we may just act out the story and become like a stalker.

Although not usually to the intensity of a stalker, most of us have had some level of stories that promise too much at the beginning of a relationship. There is a fair amount of limerence when we first meet a person we are attracted to.

This is why the wise principles of dating suggest we take our time dating and getting to know a person. Helpful hints like be sure to date through all four seasons, have a few disagreements, have your partner meet your family and friends, meet their family and friends, and travel and vacation together. These are ways to get a better understanding of your What Is of the situation.

It might be helpful to use the idea that the actual story doesn't matter, it's what the story tells you about your Inner Person Self that is the real story. I'm just saying.

Does the story tell you that you are not enough unless you are with this person? Is it a story about this person that promises to fulfill all your needs to feel loved and desired? Are you looking for this person to make you feel awake and alive? These are all stories that are from the outside of you.

Take care to look at the relationship from your inner awakeness, the awake Inner Person Self. Not from the River Mind, not from the Body Boat, but the inner seat where you sit down to watch the River Mind and inspect the Boat Body.

Fantasy is a River thing.

*   *   *

Garrett has come to sex therapy to get help as he continues to recover from prostate cancer surgery.

He reports that prior to his diagnosis of cancer, he and his life partner, Rose, had an active and satisfying sex life. At our first session, he said that they both enjoyed starting sex by watching "stories that showed the sex lives of regular people."

After each session, Garrett takes home a full report to Rose. He reports that Rose likes these new ideas so much that she has asked Garrett if she can come to his next session. "Not quite yet," he told her. "I still have some stuff to work on." After a few sessions, when we have discussed building the Intimacy Bridge, Pleasure, and Erotic flow, it seems like a good time to ask the question.

First, I check with him about what he wants to talk about.

"Some stuff" that he has worried about is how to start initiating sex again. He and Rose had tried a couple of times with their usual routine, and though he had pleasured Rose to climax, he had not been able to hold an erection.

This gives me the opportunity to ask the question that I don't like to ask.

"How often do you watch porn?" There it is. The question I don't like to ask. The question that isn't the real question. The question that, for those who are asked it, is difficult to be honest about.

I ask it like I have been trained to ask it. To bring up what might be a "hot potato" topic like porn, you ask it in a way that gives "permission" for porn. Rather than asking "Do you watch porn?" you start with a permission-giving assumption that the person watches porn.

Garrett doesn't answer the question, but he does do what is important to do. He talks about porn.

"That's what I want to talk to you about. Is porn bad to watch?" He goes on to detail that when he watches porn by himself, as he has always done, he is still able to get an erection and have a climax. He's worried that the increased use of porn he has had lately might be dulling his "attraction" to Rose.

I note that Garrett is equating his erection with attraction. This is a focus on arousal. It's like waiting for our Boat Body to somehow get to the right part of our River Mind.

I listen to the details. They are the Outside Story.

I have been asked this question many times. "Is porn bad for me?"

On the other side of the coin is the idea that porn is good. I've heard many people say, "Porn is good! Sex-positive even!" because it helps you be more skilled, build your fantasies, rev up, and be more comfortable with sexual encounters.

I will not "help" Garrett by taking a side on porn. Porn is good or porn is bad isn't going to help Garrett.

*　　*　　*

Queer Theory invites us to try the "both and" attitude. The idea that something is not necessarily either totally bad or totally good, either yes or no, but could be yes and no—both at the same time. This is "don't know what you don't know" territory.

The topic of fantasy (that's what porn is) and how that fits into sex is one of those topics where it might be easy to get hooked into "It's good!" or "It's bad!"

Fantasy can be good and fantasy can be not helpful. Let's keep both hands open.

Let's start with the good.

We have said that Fantasy is picture stories and images generated by your River Mind that your Body likes and responds to. Our Bodies remember every single thing we encounter or experience. They remember happy and feeling good moments, and they remember downer and painful moments. The body signs off on, approves of, stories that offer a solution or repair of something we need or want in life. What we fantasize about, the story that pulls us in, offers to make our unrealized dreams and wishes come true. The story soothes our pain, traumas, and feelings of isolation or neglect. In fact, we do feel better, we feel a sense of positive energy, roused with a wake-up moment in our Bodies and our Minds. Fantasy allows us to instantly thrill and connect with a story.

Fantasy is the Mind and Body asking "What if?" "What if" there is a different way this goes? We can look at the story line of a fantasy to understand and get to places that are hidden deeply with us.

If we pay attention to the story of a fantasy, we may gain an understanding of something in our life that we can address to understand ourselves and become a better more evolved version of ourselves.

Fantasy can help us connect to hidden feelings. For example, fantasy about random sex might resonate with our stories and worries about not being desirable. Fantasy about bondage, dominance, or submission might mirror our stories and concerns about feeling powerlessness, helplessness, weakness, or fear of losing control. Fantasy that depicts lovemaking, romance, and devotion might tap into our deep sense of isolation or loneliness.

Fantasy can help us pay attention to important symbols. For example, breasts might represent nurture, being taken care of. Muscles may give you the feeling of being safe and protected. Uniforms and formal dress may give you the feeling of stability, being treated well, fitting in, following what is expected.

Fantasy offers Sexual possibility or Desire fulfillment. Sudden strong attraction may feel like this person completes you; when you are with them you are okay. Something about this person makes the story of your Self feel good, or provides something (a new picture of yourself, a type of sexual experience) you feel you are lacking.

Here are some ways fantasy is not helpful:

- We seek fantasy to wake us up instead of practicing Awakeness.
- We often use fantasy to help disassociate from painful emotions and experiences.

- The fantasy of limerence, where we have the illusion, the story that the other person will complete us solve our unhappiness or make us feel good or okay. In limerence, we act as if the fantasy story is true. We intensely pursue a person (love bombing) whether that person feels the same way or not.

I continue a porn discussion with Garrett. "What is porn?" It is a story presented in various forms. We are drawn to stories that make us feel good about ourselves. But stories of ourselves are external stories about our Outside self. What happens when we look at the story from the Inner Person Self sitting inside of us?

We work on the real question. Not the question "Is porn bad or good?" but the question of why the stories are appealing to him. Did the story make him feel more at peace and Content, or did the story leave him craving for more story to keep his sense of power?

Fantasy can promise us power, a sense of competence, affirmation of sexuality, erotic arousal, and sexual ecstasy.

Garrett's wife Rose joins us at our next session. They practice building an Intimacy Bridge by starting with the Knee-to-Knee Exercise. As they experience comfort and enjoyment of the emotional, mental, and physical connection, I introduce the Yellow Light Encounters.[12] The Yellow Light Encounters offer different activities that assists the couple in practicing a 3D connection and Awake presence. The couple works on showing up to the What Is of sex, to their actual experience, not a story of their experience. For this couple, porn started to take a back seat to the enjoyment and pleasure of presence.

I've had experience with clients that get upset when discussing how porn might be a problem. They say things like, "You are a female, you wouldn't understand." "What kind of a sex therapist doesn't like porn?" "What kind of man doesn't use porn?" You get the picture.

I don't like to ask about porn because if someone isn't ready to wake up, if they use porn to manage and enter arousal in their sex life (instead of using Intimacy, Pleasure, and Erotic flow), it is more challenging for them to realize that porn may not be doing them any favors. If porn is the main way someone becomes aroused, we will work to help them enter into arousal from an awake awareness and specifically focus on how porn might be keeping them asleep.

---

12 For a description of the Yellow Light Encounters, see the Appendices.

Really, the bottom line about porn is "What do the stories you have about sex reveal about your Inner Person Self?"

Don't ask if porn is bad. It's not the right question.

PART FIVE

Awake Desire

About Desire

In my practice, the number-one reason couples seek sex therapy is "desire discrepancy." Put simply, one partner wants sex more than the other partner. Take, for example, "I don't have a libido—something is wrong with me!" or "My partner doesn't want to have sex with me—something must be wrong with them!"

This is fortunate for the couple. When a couple is so unhappy with their difference in wanting to have sex, they are more willing to brave sex therapy, they are more ready to actively seek to find what they don't know they don't know.

And it is fortunate for me as I guide them on their journey. I have found that "desire stories" don't lie very well. A "story of desire" cannot help but reveal how a person understands and views their Self.[13]

Since Desire is so central to the sexual experience, I want to discuss how we desire, how to "choose desire," and how to use "proactive desire."

This section of Desire includes:

- **Outside or Inside? Where Does Your Desire Come From?** A look at where your desire for sex comes from and the reasons you might not have desire.
- **Awake to the Erotic.** Discusses how to bring your whole Self to a sexual experience and practice "Erotic Flow."
- **Pleasure, the Back Door of Desire.** A discussion of what Pleasure is and why it is a "back door" to Desire.
- **Erotic Flow.** As you learn to engage both your Mind and Body with the help of your aware Self, you can enter Erotic Flow.
- **Passion and Chemistry.** The experience of a couple that thought they had lost their Desire, Passion, and Chemistry but really just didn't know how to show up fully.
- **The Secret.** How to avoid a common pitfall that sucks you into an unhelpful Arousal Focus.

---

13 Earlier we defined Sexuality as the stories we have about sex and what those stories tell us about our Self.

Outside or Inside

Where Does Your Desire Come From?

If you would like to increase or find your Desire for sex, it is helpful to check whether you think your Desire comes from Outside or Inside. If your stories about Desire are from outside of you, you can learn to find your Desire from inside of you. More specifically, do you have stories of Desire, or do you have experiences of Desire? Let's discuss the difference.

Let's start with "Are the stories I have about my Sexual Desire an Outside Story or an Inside Viewpoint?"

An Outside Story tells us that we have desire based on people and situations that aren't us.

"Have you seen my partner? They are hot! Of course I want to have sex so often! When we have sex, I often have to slow myself down."

To use the Boat, River, Person painting metaphor, when we use the Outside Story we see desire as something that comes along and shakes our shoulder to wake us up in our Boat.

The Outside Story of Desire usually focuses on "Are you aroused? Yes or no?" "Turned on? Yes or no?"

This checking to see if you are aroused comes from understanding yourself from Performance Self or Validation Self.

Because we are waiting for something to happen outside of us to trigger our desire, we are passive.

On the other hand, an Inside Viewpoint affirms and describes our experience of being awake and stepping into (paddling into) Desire.

"My favorite thing about sex is having it with you. I love how when we are having sex as my body is buzzing with pleasure, I look at you and realize you are with me. It's as if you feel what I feel, and I have an awareness that we are doing this intensely passionate thing together. I am always watching for times when we can have time to tune in to each other and move into sex."

An Inside Viewpoint focuses on presence and awakeness. Your Inner Person Self (not your Mind, not your Body) is the part of you that can understand and access your What Is—your particular experience of Desire.

Because we are awake and able to think about what we are thinking and scan our Body for sensation, energy, and messages, we can be proactive in moving into desire.

How do we remain "awake" and pay attention to our What Is experience? We turn our attention inward; we think about and observe our mind's thoughts and images. Secondly, and just as important, our inward focus allows us to think about and observe our Body. What is our energy level? What sensations do we notice? What messages is our Body telling us?

The Outside form of Desire is any "Desire" based on assessing ourselves from Latent, Performance, or Validation stories of Self. By outside we mean that we base our Desire (and also how we feel about ourselves) on actions and situations Outside ourselves. It boils down to letting things and people outside of you, not in your control, and maybe not even what you actually experience, determine if you "have Desire" for sex. If your situation tells you you should have desire; you strive to have desire whether or not you feel desire. You ignore what your Inner Person Self is actually experiencing. These are Outside stories and Outside markers of Desire. You can tell when it is a story about Desire (as opposed to the inside experience of Desire) when it offers an Outside version of Self.

The Inside story of Desire is when it comes from our awake Inner Person Self. This is Inside-based Desire. The Desire that comes from a person who has an awake sense of Self knows that they can paddle to Desire. They can use "Proactive Desire." When we are awake inside, we don't have to depend on anything or anyone to desire. We can step into Desire, and create Desire.

Let's look at some stories of Desire.

Latent Desire

Desire for sex is muted. Romantic desire may dominate, but may also be muted.

Your Self is "sleeping." Your "Desire" for sex is based on meeting your partner's need, fulfilling the roles of marriage, the relationship bond, and security.

Here are some Latent Desire stories:

- Sex is an important part of marriage, so I initiate when it's been too long or I see that my partner is getting grumpy.
- Men need sex, so if I want to keep my man happy, I will have sex.
- I don't like or enjoy sex.
- If my partner forces me to do something I don't enjoy, or want, then we aren't going to be able to stay together.
- If my partner is not going to try to keep sex exciting, I don't want to stay with them.
- I have sexual needs. If my partner can't meet them, then I need to move on.

Performance Desire

Desire is understood and activated by erotic/sexual standards and imprints from our Self of Origin, and ongoing cultural influences. Desire is for the wake-up experience (seeking turn-ons).

Your Self is asleep, but you have a pervasive sense of being restless and uncomfortable. Sexual arousal activities and sexual activity are used to make you feel good about yourself. You need a good arousal story to feel okay, happy, like you are making the grade. Arousal stories are a major detriment to whether you desire or not.

Here are some Performance Desire stories:

- I want my partner to want to want sex.
- I have no problem getting an erection.
- I want my partner to be willing to try new things, dress up, come onto me with intense passion, initiate sex.
- I am too fat.
- I am, we are, too old.
- I can't perform. I can't satisfy my partner.
- I don't have orgasms.
- I work hard to keep up my body and my sexy vibe.

Validation Desire

Desire is accessed by a partner (or you) wanting sex, initiating and responding to sexual initiation. With stories of validation, we become very intent on how others or our partners respond or interact with us. Our minds may become

261

turbulent and anxious. Since we rely on our sense of Self from others, it is very painful and devastating when it seems like others are not desiring (validating our desirability) sex with us.

In addition, Desire is thought of as needing to be spontaneous to show that it is real desire. Desire validation has a particularly obvious poker-like tell—a clue. It is the word "spontaneous." If someone uses the word spontaneous, they mean that to them a test of real desire is how spontaneously their partner is or is willing to be. This is why many couples put a lot of effort into helping sexual activity be spontaneous. Although spontaneity can be wonderful, if it is a requirement, it is an Outside Story.

Here are some Validation Desire stories:

- My partner never initiates sex, avoids sex.
- They are not attracted to me.
- I feel very angry when my partner turns me down for sex.
- My partner doesn't seem to ever think about sex.
- My partner initiates so often, I don't have a chance to even get in the mood to initiate.
- I just agree to have sex or deliberately pleasure my partner to get it over with and have some peace.
- When my partner has an erection, I have to have sex.
- I'm a "sex-every-day" kind of guy. It helps me focus and feel more confident for my day.

Most of us have told ourselves these kinds of stories.

Do you see the common thread of the Latent Self, Performance Self, and Validation Self Desire stories? The common thread is that you have very little say so in desiring sex. You either desire sex or you don't. Yes or no. Each story of desire makes you vulnerable to not want, not desire sex. Each of our stories tell us that the way to feel good about sex is to play our role, perform, and get validation. There is a very good chance that will not always happen.

When our Inner Person Self is awake, we don't have to rely on Outside stories to help us Desire. We can choose to Desire. We can enter "Proactive Desire." We can create Desire, and we can rest when we don't have a sense of desire. We can do this by directing our attention to waking up our Inner Person Self.

Are you ready to wake up and experience Desire?

The stories of sex that are dependent on people and situations outside of us usually don't end up working for most of us—not for the long term. So, when these stories start breaking down and don't work, what can we do about it? This is the good part. The part we didn't know we didn't know.

We have said that the first step of experiencing Desire is to start by looking inside to find and see your Self. How do you do that?

The short answer is "Wake up in your Boat."

We begin to wake up our sleepy Self by asking "What if?"

Responsive Desire

Practicing the What Is of your sexual feelings and experiences is Responsive Desire. Responsive Desire is discovered by attention to the truth of our experience. We find Responsive Desire by becoming present, being in the moment with our What Is. This is much different from waiting to go where our River Mind takes us. We look for the truth of what our experience is.

For example, "awake, responsive Desire" is not mostly a conversation we are having in our head, that increases our sexual arousal but with very little enjoyment felt in our Bodies. It is not a movie of exciting images that we see in our Minds and follow the fantasy to orgasm. Although I wouldn't call these wrong, they are not Responsive because our Inner Person Self is not awake, but sedated. Perhaps blissfully so.

Most importantly, the passive and sleepy Latent, Performance, and Validation ways of accessing Desire will inevitably not work, or not work as well, and we will begin seeking more arousal. Something will happen to make you say, "My libido isn't what it used to be," "I'm not a sexual person," "I love my partner; I'm just not in love," "Our passion is gone," or "We never had good chemistry."

Responsive Desire is discovered by engagement of the Inner Person Self (vs. thoughts of the River Mind, passive eroticism). Libido is energized and sustained by skillful Intimacy and Erotic Flow practices. We become more concerned with being present to the actual in-the-moment experience than pursuing desire. We begin to want to have sex in a way that helps us feel connected (present, awake) with our Inner Person Self and in turn connected and intimate with our partner.

The good news is that Responsive Desire allows you to have a remedy to a "I don't have Desire" situation. And it comes from your awake Inner Person Self.

Integrated Desire

Just as we have invited you to include your Self in all parts of your life and relationships, we invite you to include yourself in your sexual desires and libido. The most dependable Desire comes from the Responsive Inner Person Self and is created and reinforced by positive Pleasure and Erotic Flow experiences from the Integrated Desire view. You include your 3D Self[14] and you invite your partner to include their 3D Self in sexual activity.

So, for example, rather than trying to literally act out or follow someone's exciting erotic fantasy, you can look for the story under the fantasy. You ask about the story and find out what the story does for them. For example, imagining multi-partner sex might give a sense that "multiple people desire me, and therefore I feel really desirable." Thinking about being tied up with sexual activity, may give a sense of relief of responsibility or of not having to work so hard to perform at sex. Playing around with a taboo, dressing a part, or putting on a costume or object may take a person into new awareness in their Mind and Body that intensifies their sense of alertness, awakeness, and presence. Does it give them a sense of Desirability, a sense of power, a sense of being able to let go, a sense of heightened body ecstasy?

When we explore the story, it allows both people to come into the understanding and experience. Practicing Responsive Desire is much more sustainable than trying to recreate the immediate arousal focus that the fantasy is used for. If two people can become awake about the fantasy, it not only allows both people to start at the same place of Responsiveness, but makes it possible to act out and play with the fantasy in a more authentic and enthusiastic way.

If you want to quit worrying about or increase your desire or libido, take the Inside View.

---

14   The "3D" of Self includes emotional, mental, and physical dimensions.

Awake to the Erotic
What Is Erotic?

An erotic experience comes from a story in your Mind. That story wakes up your Body.

The word "erotic" is commonly used for people, activities, and behavior or objects that ignite sexual energy, or are associated with starting or enhancing sexual arousal. There is an infinite supply of stories. Here are some popular erotic ideas:

- Erections, lubricating
- Kissing, foreplay
- A sexy person or person posed, dressed (lingerie, leather) or acting in a sexualized way ("dirty talk," mannerisms)
- Playing a sexual fantasy in your mind, or the literal acting out of the fantasy
- Sexualized places, activities, and groups (sex in a hotel room, swinging party, frat party, bachelor party, social media such as Ashley Madison—a site that promotes "Have an affair"—"What happens in Vegas, stays in Vegas").
- Special Interest groups, events, and websites (gender bending, pony play, rope play, multiplayer platform groups, cosplay, larping, fetish)
- Porn/Erotic Media
- Romance stories
- Vibrators/sex toys
- BDSM play activities (bondage, discipline, dominance and submission, sadism, masochism)

When we want to have a more exciting and fulfilling sex life, there is a tendency to want to get a more exciting sex story. Most of us focus on "getting more in touch with our sexual self" and having more exciting sexual activities. Another way to say it is that we are seeking to be more aroused and feel more aroused.

We pursue sexual activity by adding or focusing on more sexy, erotic thoughts—more arousal. We paddle to exciting parts of our River Minds. This does work and is quite enjoyable for many people for lengthy amounts of time. However, focusing on arousal is not a place of Contentment. If we are always needing to keep things fresh, experience new stories, or test our personal limits in order to be at our best sexually, then when will we ever be able to rest? To just be? To be awake and present and alive?

In our metaphor of the "Boat. River. Person. painting," when we think about the Erotic, it is helpful to include attention to the Boat. Our Body. Although we all notice the arousal of our Bodies, most of us depend on arousal that starts in our Mind. Erotic Energy comes from activities that match and resonate with our sexuality imprints and emotional stories and cause the Body to wake up (turn on, become sexually aroused, experience enhanced arousal). Our Mind leads out in the experience.

If we stay, or rather let our River Minds take us wherever they will, we tend to focus ever more tightly on the sexual energy and our attention is hyper-focused on that energy.

If you want to increase your erotic energy and sexual arousal, you can attend to—become Responsive, awake, and present to—your whole Body.

By "attend," I do not mean that you make sure your body looks a certain way, that you act or respond in a way that shows passionate, turned-on desire. With your attention to the Boat Body, there is less need for the right kind of turn-on, medication, supplements, or surgery to get it to act a certain way.

I also don't mean for you to focus on your arousal—but rather pay attention to the whole Body. Be present to the whole Body. This is a deliberate way of directing your Mind to pay attention to what the Body is communicating. This is a fine line of distinction. Some of us try to engage erotic triggers from only what is in the River Mind; some of us think that anything that gets us wanting to have sex is great and we enjoy riding the Body sensations into a "high" of ecstasy.

A good way to determine if we are awake in our erotic experiences is to figure out if we are in the moment or in the stories of our Minds. Are we following the thoughts or are we following the experience of being in our Body?

We will discuss how to be more fully present in the chapters in Part Six. In regards to being more fully present with erotic energy, three ways to do that are to check the meaning of arousal, do a Body scan, and engage your senses.

Check the meaning

Each time you are awakened, aroused, or energized, your Body is sharing some important information with you. Things turn you on because they are something your Body "remembers" as pleasant, pleasurable, helpful, healing, or matching your stories of sex (and view of Self!). If you look even more closely, you can see that what turns you on, represents or gives you a sense of things like power, belonging, desirability, worthiness, "okayness," aliveness.

Body Scan

A "Body scan" is to focus from head to toe to check for any sensations. It is common when a person is sexually aroused that they focus in on the sexually energized parts of their Body and lean into and work to increase those pleasurable feelings. Rather than focusing exclusively on enhancing sexual arousal, direct your attention to pleasurable sensations throughout your whole Body. For example, your face, your hands, your feet.[15]

Enjoyment and Engagement of your senses

Our sensuality is our ability (like a USB port on a computer) to get and give information and to get and give energy. Each of our senses[16] can be a source of enjoyment and add to our Awake sexual experience.

When you think of your erotic ideas, whether you are adventuresome or not, open to anything or not, queer or not, kinky or not, vanilla/chocolate or not—whatever your story or experience is, I invite you to Wake Up to your What Is during a sexual experience.

The Views of Self—Latent, Performance, Validation, Responsive, and Integrated—are very helpful in understanding what sparks excitement for us and how to tap deeply into your own eroticism. Your most developed sense of eroticism is

---

15 For pleasuring men, it may be helpful to start pleasuring the genitalia and erogenous zones first and then expanding the pleasuring to the whole body in order to arouse the whole body. For pleasuring women, try pleasuring the whole body and working to expand the pleasure to the genitalia and erogenous zones in order to arouse the whole body.

16 Smell, Touch, Taste, Sound, Sight, Rhythm, Proprioception (awareness of body in space and movements and strength needed to complete at action), Vestibular (sense of balance, coordination, and orientation to space), Interoception (awareness of internal bodily states).

likely not what you think it is, but goes back to how awake you are in your Boat Body on your River Mind.

The secret to a deeper eroticism is to wake up. Think about what your erotic thoughts are and scan and be present to your whole Body. This is different than just going wherever the story in your River Mind takes your Boat Body.

Erotic Awakeness

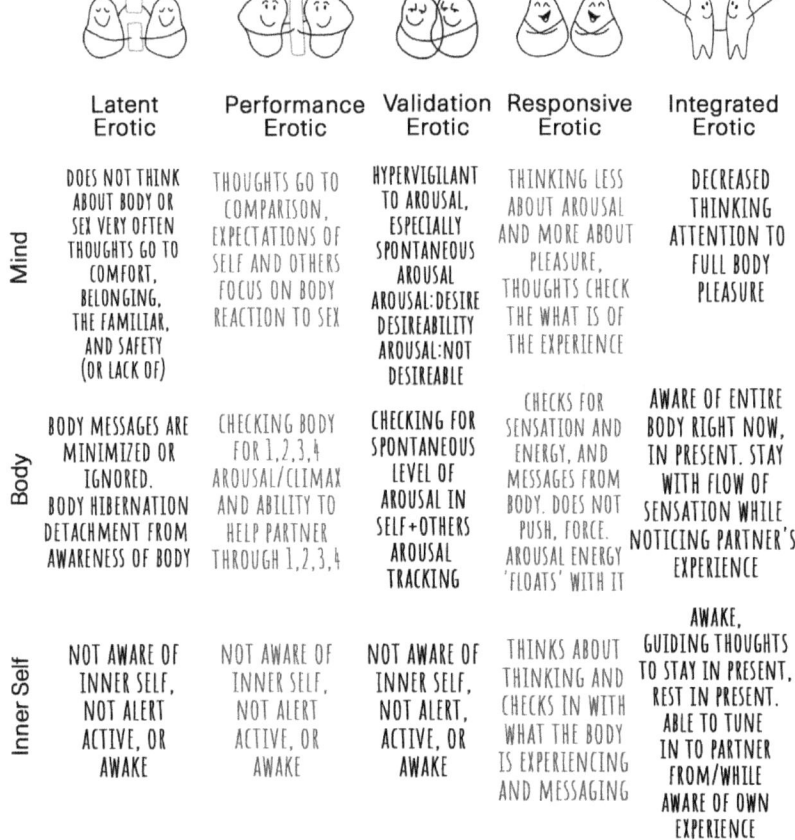

	Latent Erotic	Performance Erotic	Validation Erotic	Responsive Erotic	Integrated Erotic
Mind	DOES NOT THINK ABOUT BODY OR SEX VERY OFTEN THOUGHTS GO TO COMFORT, BELONGING, THE FAMILIAR, AND SAFETY (OR LACK OF)	THOUGHTS GO TO COMPARISON, EXPECTATIONS OF SELF AND OTHERS FOCUS ON BODY REACTION TO SEX	HYPERVIGILANT TO AROUSAL, ESPECIALLY SPONTANEOUS AROUSAL AROUSAL:DESIRE DESIREABILITY AROUSAL:NOT DESIREABLE	THINKING LESS ABOUT AROUSAL AND MORE ABOUT PLEASURE, THOUGHTS CHECK THE WHAT IS OF THE EXPERIENCE	DECREASED THINKING ATTENTION TO FULL BODY PLEASURE
Body	BODY MESSAGES ARE MINIMIZED OR IGNORED. BODY HIBERNATION DETACHMENT FROM AWARENESS OF BODY	CHECKING BODY FOR 1,2,3,4 AROUSAL/CLIMAX AND ABILITY TO HELP PARTNER THROUGH 1,2,3,4	CHECKING FOR SPONTANEOUS LEVEL OF AROUSAL IN SELF+OTHERS AROUSAL TRACKING	CHECKS FOR SENSATION AND ENERGY, AND MESSAGES FROM BODY. DOES NOT PUSH, FORCE. AROUSAL ENERGY 'FLOATS' WITH IT	AWARE OF ENTIRE BODY RIGHT NOW, IN PRESENT. STAY WITH FLOW OF SENSATION WHILE NOTICING PARTNER'S EXPERIENCE
Inner Self	NOT AWARE OF INNER SELF, NOT ALERT ACTIVE, OR AWAKE	NOT AWARE OF INNER SELF, NOT ALERT ACTIVE, OR AWAKE	NOT AWARE OF INNER SELF, NOT ALERT, ACTIVE, OR AWAKE	THINKS ABOUT THINKING AND CHECKS IN WITH WHAT THE BODY IS EXPERIENCING AND MESSAGING	AWAKE, GUIDING THOUGHTS TO STAY IN PRESENT, REST IN PRESENT. ABLE TO TUNE IN TO PARTNER FROM/WHILE AWARE OF OWN EXPERIENCE

Pleasure
It's a Body Thing

Pleasure is a message from your Body that shifts and directs your Mind to focus on something that feels good. Your Body is giving you a wake-up message.

In the last chapter we discussed how the Erotic starts in the Mind to wake up the Body. Pleasure works the other way around. Pleasure starts in the Body and communicates to the Mind. Pleasure is sensations and expressions of enjoyment that come from our Body. Pleasure wakes up and speaks to our Mind.

Just as many people use the word "intimacy" or "desire" and may not pay attention to their actual What Is, the meaning of the word Pleasure can also vary from story to story. It might be a way of talking about feeling good feelings in your Body, sexual arousal, or sex.

We can access our Desire for sexual experiences by starting with Pleasure. Pleasure is a form of "Proactive Desire." This intentional, "awake" Desire happens when you start by focusing on finding Pleasure in the Body. It even works to remember a pleasurable experience.

You can decide that you will seek a pleasurable sensation or experience in your Body. You can decide to focus on doing activities that make your Body feel good. Proactive Desire is an Inside way of engaging in Pleasure and, if you want, inviting the Mind to a sexual experience. You can intentionally start with Pleasure and invite the Mind to join in.

Examples of Pleasure and Proactive Experiences of Pleasure
- **Choose Delight and Fun** Body Response: Laugh, smile
- **Choose thoughts**[17] **or memories of Delight, Fun, and Enjoyment** Body Response: Smile, heightened energy in chest and stomach

---

17 Our memory is stored in our brain, which is a Body part. Our Mind is that River of words, thoughts, images, ideas that flows through our awareness at all times.

- **Choose activities and/or thoughts or memories of Peace, Rest, Security** Body Response: Sigh, Spontaneous breath and relaxation
- **Choose activities and/or thoughts or memories of Exciting and Pleasure-Filled Sex** Body Response: Heightened energy in genitalia and erogenous parts of body
- **Choose Body Movement** Body Response: Rhythmic movement, translative movement (moving in response to sound or thoughts), repetitive flow movement (tasks, activities), and social movement (dancing, walking, running, attending an event like a concert or ballgame with another person or a crowd of people, moving without thought, moving in sync with another person, movement that is connected to your inner experience).
- **Choose Sensuality, Engagement, and Enjoyment of Our Senses** Touch, Taste, Smell, Sight, Sound, Kinesthetics (tuning in to the sensations of your body movement, balance, and position).
- **Choose Person to Person (Self to Self) Contact, Intimacy** Eye gazing feels good and comfortable to maintain. Feels in synch, without worry or effort. Can rest in the moment with your partner. You can see your partner seeing you see them.

When a person has quit, does not want to, or has never responded to Outside forms of Desire and Arousal—"Erotic Energy wake-ups," Pleasure is a way to find Desire to enjoy and engage the Body and move into sexual activity if you want to.

We can deliberately wake up the Body and "paddle" to turn our attention to sexual enjoyment while still staying present to our Body. When you are able to float, and to be present with full What Is presence in Mind and Body, you can more easily enter into Pleasure or Erotic flow.

Secrets of the Erotic
Responsive Eroticism

When you think of the word "erotic," what comes to mind?

A Dominatrix wearing leather? Handcuffs? Plunging necklines? Tight asses? Dreamy jawlines? Someone fervently and insistently desiring and wanting sex with you? Sex that colors outside the mainstream (or your personal) lines? Something that gets you turned on for sex? Alter ego play?

Whatever your thoughts or definitions of erotic, they are connected to your stories of sex. It bears repeating that our stories of sex may not be what we actually experience and the stories always reveal valuable information about our understanding of our Self.

In the first part of this book, I shared that in therapy, I point out to my clients that Intimacy is not sex. You can have sex that is intimate, and you can have sex that has very little intimacy as a part of the experience.

The same goes for the erotic. Sex is not eroticism. You can have sex that is erotic, and you can have sex that has very little eroticism as a part of the experience.

How can you tell? Isn't sexual arousal an erotic experience?

Yes, partly.

When we desire to have sex, anything that arouses us, gives us a wake-up moment is erotic. Sexual arousal is erotic in that we have and use arousing behaviors, people, and things to get turned on. These wake-up moments where you focus on your pleasure energy and you closely follow your sexual arousal until you release in orgasm are started with the erotic. A story in your Mind that wakes up the Body.

When we want to have sex, we tend to focus on our arousal and climax. That's normal. We pursue arousal to wake up and focus more and more tightly to heightened sexual energy. We focus, ride, and release ourselves to the arousal energy and orgasm. The experience is guided by our River Minds. We (our Inner Person Self) snooze as our Boat Body gets pulled over the "waterfall" of climax. It feels great.

Let's walk through that sex experience again. We notice that we have a wake-up moment of arousal. We feel our Body shift and move to the arousal energy—get turned on. Where is our attention? If we are focused on the story in our Mind, our gaze follows a spiraling inward path. Awakeness recedes as our River Mind pulls us along in the current of the story. Our attention is drawn like a magnet to the energy, and we gladly watch it and float on it. As we ride along on this strong current of energy from our Mind to our sexual parts, we barely notice the rest of our Body. This is normal. It feels good, but it is not Erotic Flow.

Our Minds can spark the erotic and tell the exciting arousing story, but it is in being in, experiencing our entire Body that we enter a sustained Erotic Flow. We can only fully awaken in our Body when our Inner Person Self is paying attention. In other words, we, the Person in the Boat on the River, are awake.

An Erotic Flow experience starts with a different intention. The goal is to practice staying awake and being present. You do that by staying with the pleasure of the whole Body for the entire experience. An Erotic Flow experience is when your River Mind, Boat Body, and Inner Person Self are awake. Alive. The focus is on feeling deeply connected to your whole painting Self.

The erotic experience that flows does so because we are awake when we approach erotic wake-ups. We practice staying present and awake in the moment both in arousal and the sexual activities and as we approach orgasm and after. The experience happens in our Boat Body. We are able to watch our thoughts and at the same time keep our attention, tune in to and experience sensations in our Body. We are present in our Body, taking in all the sensations along with the sexual energy. We are able to position ourselves on our high seats above the River, allowing the current of our Mind to flow under us instead of sweeping us along. We think less, have fewer words as we enter more fully into the sensations and messages of our Body. This is because our Inner Person Self is awake and present.

Our personal eroticism is always going to reflect our stories of our Self. Do we understand our sexual selves in a Latent, Performance, or Validation way? To become more erotic, we notice those stories as we turn our focus to what it feels like in our Body. This is becoming Responsive to the What Is of our erotic experience.

I see a hand up for a question.

"But isn't that the point of a sexual experience? Isn't it pleasurable to let go, go with the story and release to the sexual experience?"

Good question. The answer is that it is not a "yes or no, either or" situation. It is a "both and" answer. To understand how to embrace eroticism more deeply, you can think of it as a two-handed experience, and a "both and" practice. Yes, you can follow the excitement of the arousal process with full abandon and yes, you can practice being awake while having sex. This allows you to move from the arousal focus to a more "What Is my experience?" approach.

It is exciting to understand Awake Eroticism because it allows for each human person to move from their stories of their sexuality(arousal focus and arousal hyper-focus, broken, not sexual, not interested, highly sexual, not happy, really open to sex, sex positive) to their own authentic experience of Sexuality. Their Sexuality Counts—because their Inner Person Self always, always Counts.

Erotic Flow
Awake-Awake

A wonderful thing can happen when you start becoming awake and Responsive in your sexuality, sex experiences, and relationship. You will be able to experience Erotic Flow. Erotic Flow allows you and your partner to have a sustained time of being fully present with each other during sex. You are dialed in. The Intimacy Bridge is open. You are attuned, your attention is clicked into the present so that your arousal, pleasure, and movements are effortless.

This is not something you can Perform. It is something you experience because it requires your full presence. This isn't the ultimate level of lovemaking, because it isn't something most people learn how to do and then do it every time. Erotic Flow is a result of the practice of Awakeness and presence in Intimacy and sex.

Here are some examples of Erotic Flow:

A euphoric high experienced during sex—not just with orgasm. Like a runner's high or burst of creative inspiration, you and your partner have a rhythm with intercourse that feels smooth and effortless, you are in tune to the rhythm. You stop thinking, but you are fully awake and alive. You feel like you could, would like to, stay here forever.

Sentient presence. A connection with another living being, usually felt with messages received with eye contact. Feeling seen in a way that helps you understand the other person more fully. You can see your partner seeing you see them.

A feeling of opening/openness. You feel your partner's comforting presence and reassuring attention to you. Which in turn causes a sensation of mentally and physically opening up to and receiving pleasurable human connection and sexual energy.

Message sent, message received. You intentionally send emotional (grateful, cherished, beloved, I want you, I desire you) and physical messages (tenderness, energetic intensity, unhurried caressing, focused attention to parts of body, confident rhythmic touches) to your partner by full attention and awareness of how you touch your partner and you can feel their body and energy respond to you.

Solo Erotic Flow, when pleasuring self. Focus your attention into the present moment. This may include eyes open and attention to breath to focus and quiet the thoughts in your Mind. Think of starting from the inside Inner Person Self; "sit in the up-high seat of your Inner awareness," and invite your Mind and Body along. Affirm yourself by thinking caring, beautiful, and grateful thoughts. Notice and touch all parts of your body. Allow and experiment with the ebb and flow of arousal by alternating genital stimulation, scanning, and touching all parts of your Body. What message is your Body sending you? Comfort? Sadness? Reassurance? Joy? Soothing? Anxiety? The best way to access your Full Mind and Body Arousal is to keep your eyes open and stay present in the moment. Yes, keeping your eyes open even if you are going solo.

If fantasy imagery is a part of your arousal, try thinking about the fantasy as if you were watching it from afar. What do you notice about the story? Experiment with switching from the fantasy you are having in your head to tuning in to your body's pleasurable sensations and increase those. If you use fantasy to start your arousal, experiment with "putting it on the shelf." This is a phrase I use to help people direct their attention away from an image or idea. I have them picture themselves scooping up the thought and placing it on a shelf in their mind. Think of it as setting it aside to take out later if you want it. This opens space to experience your Self in a different way. Go slowly and alertly, don't be in a rush to move on from observing and listening to your Body and Mind.

Kink Flow. The stories of Kink play can move you into a full Body and full attention state. Whatever the story being played out (e.g., bondage, dominance, intense immersive Body sensations), the flow happens Inside when you "get up in your chair" high above your River Mind and drop into your Boat Body. You stay present in the experience, your Inner Person Self wakes up to the What Is of the moment.

Eroticism is a story that transports and shifts your awareness from the current of your Mind into your Body. The energy awakens you to your Body and Inner Person Self's Intense aliveness and energy.

Passion and Chemistry
Throw a Party?

Rakesh and Sheva are a married, same-sex couple that have come to the point where they are worried about their sex life. The men care very much for each other and yet the passion that brought them together and made them so excited for a future has disappeared.

I notice they look at each other as they speak as if to include and support their partner in this therapy journey. They easily take turns telling their story. Rakesh says he wants me to know that they are the best of friends. Sheva shares they feel they have a blessed and good life together.

When there is a pause, I join the conversation. "What is your hope for our work here?"

Sheva answers, "We have lost our passion, our chemistry. We don't do erotic things anymore."

Rakesh remains quiet.

Sheva continues. He tells how he has tried many times to talk about why they are not having sex. Yet the conversation always goes the same way.

"Rakesh will say it's because of stress. He says when he gets stressed with his job, he feels so much pressure that sex is the last thing he needs to think about. Sometimes he says he is afraid he will disappoint me and not satisfy what I need in sex."

Sheva continues, "For my part, I suspect that Rakesh is not attracted to me anymore. If I am honest, I sometimes wonder if I am attracted to him. I know one thing for sure, when Rakesh will not talk about sex, and is so passive about our sex life, I feel rejected. I want to know that my partner feels attracted to me, and is able to rise above his tough times to have a sex life with me. I have been over and over this. I know we don't have the chemistry and I am very afraid that we won't get it back."

Rakesh finally speaks. "I have tried to add some spark, some erotic scenarios back and plan romantic evenings, but they often feel awkward." He turns to Sheva, "Let's be honest, the last time I initiated, you turned me down."

Sheva shares that they have a way that they like to start up sex that has worked for them really well for a long time. "One of us starts the kissing. And I mean intense—don't let your partner go kind of kissing! Usually in the kitchen. And that's our way to start having sex right then and there!"

I understand how I can help this couple.

I sometimes wish I could tell my clients, "You haven't lost your chemistry or your passion, you just don't understand how they work."

But that wouldn't be very good therapy.

I look at Rakesh as I start with the "What if?"

"What if you invite Sheva to do something with your bodies that you could enjoy?"

The look on both their faces says, "Huh?"

"Like what would happen if you sat in a chair and invited Sheva to come sit on your lap?" I offer.

Rakesh glances at Sheva. "I'm not sure. I don't remember ever having him sit on my lap."

I continue with some "What ifs." "What if Sheva really likes being held? What if you really like it? What if you don't? Let's find out."

They go home to explore the "What is?" of deliberately holding and being held.

*   *   *

Three weeks pass and Rakesh and Sheva return for another session. Sheva enthusiastically reports that they have done the exercise and he loves it.

I check in with Rakesh. "How did you like it?"

"It was nice. It got us to try something new and spend some time together that was about just being together."

I take them back through what the experience was like for them. I guide them to think about their experience by checking on how they felt in their Body.

A long and rich discussion unfolds. I notice that they both spend time talking about how it felt in their Body to be held.

In contrast to jumping into sex as soon as they had the "erection go-ahead," Rakesh said, "I realize I am usually so intent on having sex, using my erection and satisfying Sheva, that I don't think about me or my Body. It's as if we are so focused on sex that we aren't with each other. Being held and being able to relax back into his arms was the most peaceful I have felt in some time."

Sheva is eager to join in. "I am still surprised at how great it felt. It felt like we were in our own world. I felt like Rakesh was not distracted and was fully with me."

Both continue to talk with new enthusiasm.

Rakesh and Sheva have begun their journey to be Responsive to their Self and to Integrate their Self into every part of the relationship—including sexual encounters. They are starting to listen to what the Body is saying to them. They are showing up as whole people. They are not trying to start a sexual experience without their Body. They are awake and listening to what their Mind is telling them and what their Bodies are messaging them.

Although we are just starting and there is more work to do, I'm not worried about them having enough chemistry or passion. They are on their way to practicing this "Boat Thing" and practicing entering into Erotic Flow in their sexual experiences.

The Secret
Both Hands

Rakesh and Sheva were upfront and able to speak about their worry that the passion in their sex life was gone.

But often this worry of chemistry and passion is a secret that someone keeps to themselves.

Over the years, many clients have brought their sex secret to me. It makes sense to bring the secret to someone who is helping you with your sex life.

I usually learn about the secret because after a few couples sessions, one partner will contact me and ask me for an individual session. My policy is, if at all possible, to work for several sessions as a couple in order to get both partners fully engaged and working as quickly as possible. I also discourage secrets, and if I am told one, I strongly encourage the partner to tell their partner. So, when someone asks for an individual session, I ask if they have let their partner know that they will have an individual session. I'm stricter about this than I used to be because I've had my share of oopsies.

Secrets have a tendency to escape in surprising ways, and working with couples, I am the one left holding the bag with the angry kitty using their claws. A receipt for counseling services sent to a home address. A slightly guilty look in a partner's eyes, or my own reference to what seems a safe detail about the secret individual session. It doesn't take much to cause a loss of trust in me and my ability to help. Scenarios like these are often irreparable.

The secret about chemistry and passion sounds like, "I am not attracted to my partner. Please don't tell them. It would really hurt them."

It's a heavy burden to feel like you are not interested in having sex with your partner. But it isn't irreparable, and it's not that hard to move on from. This is why I don't like the word "chemistry." The "You either have it or not" viewpoint. Yes or no.

Exactly what are you referring to? What tells you that you are attracted to your partner?

"Wanting to have sex, to kiss, to touch, and be physical with them."

Hmm.

"When I see someone who I am attracted to, I immediately feel sexually aroused."

"It makes me want to have sex with them, to think of having sex with them."

"Sexual attraction gives me tunnel vision and tunnel attention. I don't easily shake off the images and the energy that the person sparks in me."

These ideas of attraction and chemistry are all based on the story of waiting for your Body to get aroused, waiting for your Mind to tell you a story and wake up your Body.

The idea of "both and, both can be true" is more helpful. What if you tried, "I am not attracted to my partner at the moment and I want to learn how to choose arousal."

You don't have to sit around waiting to be aroused and be interested. That is the "Closed," sleepy self, asking "How to do sex," the 1, 2, 3, 4 story about sex.

PART SIX

Awake Sex

How to Do Sex

1, 2, 3, 4

Sex scenes in TV shows and movies tell us how to have sex. What to do.

It is basically a four-step process—a 1, 2, 3, 4 story.

Step 1. Interest. You show focused and intense interest in each other. This happens either by unflinching eye contact or by some clever play on words. "I think we need to talk—privately." "Would you show me your new car?" This intense focus means you are sexually attracted to one another.

Step 2. Kissing. Quite often, two people suddenly lunge toward each other like magnets and start kissing. In another variation, one person starts kissing the unsuspecting other person. The startled person pauses for a moment, may open their eyes, but then fervently returns the kiss.

Step 3. Doing sexual things. Touching all over. Clothes coming off. Once there is a clear message sent back and forth by enthusiastic kissing, then it is time to take clothes off and touch all the special parts. Touch them and energize. Fan the sparks of the awakening genitals and parts of the body.

Step 4. Orgasm. Goal achieved.

For a TV or movie scene, the doing sexual things and orgasm usually is suggested by waking up in the same bed, clothes all over the floor, and what the couple says or doesn't say to each other in the morning. Also, one of two things happens because you had sex. Either you are now a couple (if you are already a couple, you are happy with each other), or you are not a couple and are not happy you had sex.

Interest. Check.

Kissing. Check.

Doing sexual things. Check.

Orgasm. Check. "We have had sex."

This is a pretty blunt list. We would hope to add a bit of finesse and skill to the endeavor. Yet, most of us have that same list in our minds. We may have never thought of it as a checklist. But we follow it when we are having sex with another person. It is a script in our head about how sex should go. Most significantly, when I draw this on my whiteboard, I point out that we feel that if we get to step 4, we have had sex.

We can add notes to that script. Stage instructions for what we need to do to bring out the best story. But we basically proceed with 1, 2, 3, 4.

Sexual arousal is a wake-up moment. We notice a strong energy in our genitals that we can't ignore. It is a moment when our Inner Person Self has their eyes open and is paying attention to what the Body has to say. Our Mind is focused on these pleasurable sensations spreading over our whole Body. We want more. Like starting a fire, we intensely focus and fan every bit of pleasure.

Maybe we pace ourselves artfully by slowly adding more and more sensation; or we ramp up to full-on energy to intensify the sensation. Slow and tender, or wild and unrestrained, all out, everything you got. Maybe a back and forth to both.

You receive this wake-up call of your River Mind, and Body Boat, and you are swept along. The flow of energy quickens you. You are willing and wanting to go where it takes you.

You close your eyes to focus on how the sexual pleasure is increasing. There is nothing else except the delicious and mesmerizing pleasure energy.

Suddenly you notice a surge of pleasurable energy. Can you stand it? It's like coming to the surface after a deep dive. Your Body shudders and you take the biggest breath you can. You take a leap and lean into the energy for more intensity.

Or maybe getting to orgasm is more like being swept to the brink of a waterfall. You pause a beat and then over the brink you fly and for a few seconds you are airborne, weightless. You float in flight to the river below.

Words do not do the arousal and orgasm experience justice. At any rate, the goal, the climax, is an orgasm. A moment of wholeness, clarity, and a deep sense of presence. Your Mind, Body, and Self are one. Whole. Alive.

Most of us don't really have a list in our head. Yet most of us do follow the 1, 2, 3, 4 idea.

Having Sex | How to do Sex

CLOSED SEX EXPERIENCE

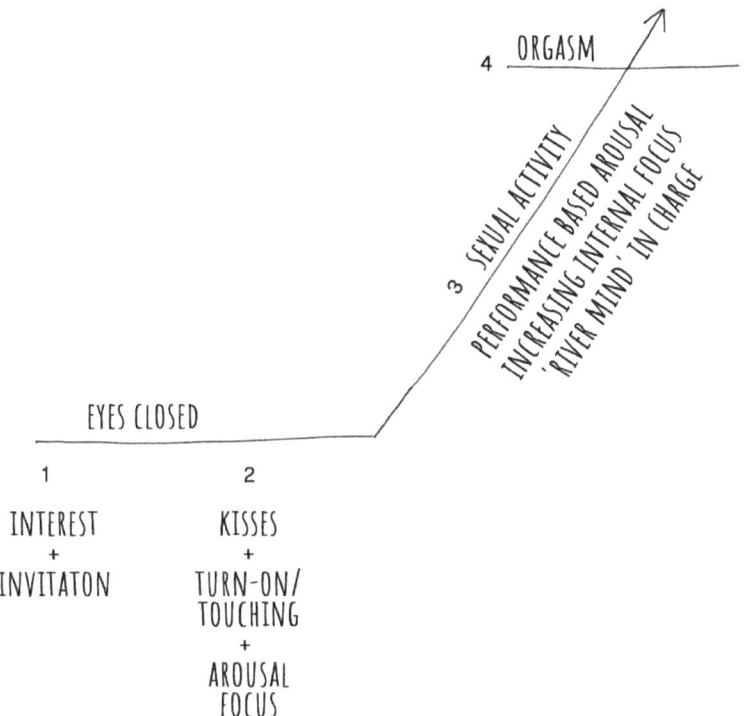

How to do sex. This list guides you through the experience, in order to be a good partner, in order to feel the pleasure of orgasm. There are an infinite number of variations to the four steps. How you show interest, whether you kiss or not, how undressed you get, where you have the encounter, how long before you orgasm or if you orgasm. You get the idea.

How to do sex. Basic information that we learn and follow, and enjoy, and don't think about very much. We get it, we know how it works.

Here's the thing: This list of how to have sex isn't the best story. It is like a red herring used to train hunting dogs. It can distract attention from the real issue. The 1, 2, 3, 4 list is an Outside Self thing and it has two issues that make it vulnerable to quit working.

First, your list of how to do sex is arousal- and performance-based. It is a linear process. First 1, then 2, then 3, and 4. The how you start sex, who you start it with, how you have sex, and how you think of your sex life. The performance of the step-by-step doing of sex is watched very closely. Aroused? Increasing arousal? Will I be able to orgasm? The focus is turned to riding the arousal energy or in watching your partner to see if they are going to make it to Step 4. Orgasm. If the ordered process gets interrupted in some way—say, the sexual activity is not getting you to number 4—it causes worry and anxiety. It pulls you into thinking and more thinking (River) about your partner's interest in sex. It distracts you and lessens your ability to be in the present moment.

Secondly, although getting sexually aroused and having a climax can be a brief moment of wake-up, this list is missing a very important something. It is missing you. The Inner Person Self. The person in the Boat who is awake and can paddle the Boat where you want to go. The Inner Person Self who is able to be present and awake in the moment.

If you are a human, sooner or later the list won't work for you. Whether you follow it alone or with another person. Your Boat Body will begin to complain about the list. Your River Mind will trick you and carry you away to places you don't like or want to go. Worry, anxiety, obsessive thoughts, feeling broken, feeling undesirable, feeling dead. All of which may make you not want to think about the list at all; or on the other side of response, make you more desperate to do the list, make it work.

Just remember when the list starts to get wonky, when it doesn't help you have sex, when it just plain doesn't get you to the goal of orgasm, it's time to ask "What if?" and look for what you don't know you don't know. You are getting an invitation to go from an Outside understanding of your Self to the wisdom of your Inner Person Self.

Wanting to Want Sex
Fed Up with Sex

The email was a long one. Erica's friend had told her to contact me for an appointment.

Dear Dr. Terrell,

My friend Jessica told me that I should talk to you. Are you accepting new patients? Here's why I need your help. My husband and I have been married 26 years and we have two teenagers, 15 and 17. I have decided that I don't like sex and don't want to have it anymore. I have told my husband about the not liking sex part, but not the part about hoping we can just not do sex at all. I know I am not the only woman that loves her husband and doesn't like sex. I've talked to my girlfriends and two of them have the same thing. Including my lesbian friend. My husband has not ever been happy with our sex life, and obviously I haven't either. I have told him that I get really stressed out when it's been a while since we've had sex, because I see him getting irritable and more needy. He suddenly wants to spend time with me even though he hasn't asked me a question in days. He starts touching me a lot and still doesn't talk. Vacations and holidays also are a problem because I always dread that he will want to have sex. I don't like to see him upset. He has told me many times that touching is his love language. It is not mine. I didn't grow up that way. It isn't something that I even think about. For many years, I have tried to be a good sex partner and have sex. I have sex when he wants to have sex. If I am honest, that is partially true, I have learned to go to bed early or how to "innocently" avoid his advances. I can tell when he wants to have sex. But the experience is never enjoyable. I feel so lonely moving my body in rhythm to him, and helping him have sex so he can get off. I'm getting older now and sex doesn't make me happy. I think that every other part of our marriage and life together is working or going in the right direction. Why should I continue to

stress about sex when it does not feel good? We are in couples therapy. Ted has told our therapist that "he wants me to want sex." That really makes me angry. He is ignoring what I want so that he can get what he wants. Besides that, I don't want the sex we have. Do you think you can helps us?

Erica's email outlines her and her husband's stories about sex. Although the stories seem to show a serious incompatibility, Erica is actually leading her husband to a new place. She is doing it right. Her recent clarity that she doesn't enjoy sex—that it doesn't feel good—is a great start to "What is?" She is waking up. She is waking up despite the couple's story. She is waking up despite her suspicion that something is wrong with her husband because of how he is "obsessed" with sex.

Erica thinks she is giving up on sex. I think it is more that she is giving up on how to do sex. She has started her journey to show up for sex. She's just getting to the good part.

I can't wait to have Erica and Ted in my office and start the party.

The Real Story of Doing Sex
Sleeping, Not Awake

We have defined Sexuality as the stories we have about sex and what those stories tell us about our Inner Person Self.

We can hear what Erica and Ted's story tells about their understanding of Self. Erica knows how to do sex—the "1, 2, 3, 4" story of how to do sex. She knows what to do.

If we made a painting of her during a sexual experience, a picture of her Boat Body floating on her River Mind, when we looked at the Person Self seated in the Boat, we would see her slumped over and deeply asleep. Her understanding of her sexual Self is Latent. She also does the Performance role as a sexual partner. She follows the 1, 2, 3, 4 plan to show him he's lovable.

It isn't so much that her "wanting to want" is missing. She, her Inner Person Self, is missing.

Doing sex is an Outside Self thing. As long as we do sex as a Role, Performance, or Validation, we are missing the real experience because we are sleeping and unresponsive.

Although Ted wants sex, he isn't awake for sex either. We know this because he isn't paddling his own Boat, he is not Responsive to his Inner Person Self. He doesn't love or accept himself as desirable and so he needs to get that sense of "okayness" from Erica. His understanding of his sexual self is based on Validation. His insistence on Erica wanting to want sex is a Performance- and Validation-level understanding of self. And Erica is not going to perform in sex any longer.

Each of us, each human, has a birthright. Because we were born and live we have a lifetime pass, a lifetime appointment, a lifetime title. It means we are lovable, worthy, desirable, okay. No matter what the River says to you, it can't take away from your worthiness, the honor of living. Until you wake up and find, become Responsive to your solid sense of worth and value, you will always be missing. Missing in sex. Missing in relationships. Drifting wherever your River Mind takes your Boat Body while your Inner Person Self is slumped there fast asleep.

Painful Sex

Messages from the Body

In our discussions of doing and having sex, I have been pointing out that when we have a 1, 2, 3, 4 plan—a story of how a sexual experience should go—two things happen. First, we put our attention on and strive for sexual arousal, which is largely a River thing. Second, as we have sex we turn our gaze, our attention, ever further inward in order to savor and get the most out of arousal from our body. This can work just fine, and does for many people. That is, until something interrupts arousal.

Pain can happen.

Pain is a message from the Body. Our wise Bodies are always watching out to protect us. When you or your partner have pain or burning more than once or twice during sex, both your Body and your River Mind start a story about it. You and your partner each have your own story. I've noticed that it is rare that partners actually discuss their stories with each other. The gist of most stories is "something is wrong with the person who is having pain." Let's be clear, it's the pain that is wrong. Full attention should be given to the pain to find out what the pain is telling us. I repeat, pain **does not** mean "something is wrong with the *person*."

The majority of those who contact me for help with painful sex are women. But men also have pain from conditions like Peyronie's disease and prostate conditions.

In 2011, I put together a program to assist in the assessment of genital and sexual pain. It included extensive assessments about what exactly happened before experiencing the pain, the kind of pain and sensations, and how the client had tried to alleviate it. After someone had completed the assessment, I provided a roadmap report to assist in diagnosing the pain and what to do about it.

In addition to counseling, one-on-one education, and group classes about sexuality, it included referrals to gynecologists, dermatologists, urologists, and physical therapists who were pelvic floor specialists.

I did the marketing thing. My messaging was "Let's figure out why these men and women have pain and assist them in healing and enjoying their sex lives again!" My office staff did mailings, newsletters, and complimentary lunch-and-learns in the doctors' offices. I had a posting program, put my toe in the "new new" of social media, which at that time was Facebook. And in case it isn't clear, the complimentary was provided by me. I "invested" a lot of money into this program.

This Road Map for Sexual Pain Assessment—refining it, training others to administer it, and getting the word out about it—was my major focus at the time. I knew it was different, but helpful, and so I was determined to inspire medical professionals and clients to make use of it.

After two years, I only had a few women who completed the assessment, and I had talked to one male client about it. An unflinching look at my return on investment and my depleted finances revealed the sad truth. The program wasn't working.

Looking back, I know I did provide some good assistance with my support, knowledge, and connecting people to referrals. My counseling with individuals and couples was solid, and I know I helped people.

The thing I didn't know I didn't know was that the program was missing a better, more effective story. I was using the Medical Model to help people who had painful sex. I am not a medical doctor and I have become way less than trusting of the medical model to address problems. Although I am very grateful that doctors know how to help the body function—or in the words of this book, work on our Boat Bodies to keep them afloat—I now know that my job is to focus on the whole painting.

The work and ultimate shelving of the "Painful Sex Road Map" was like a pricey post-graduate program that honed my knowledge and competency to help clients with painful sex.

I began to get back into my lane of my work. I realized that no amount of medications, procedures, or lubrication can effectively help someone who does not listen to their Body. And though it had its positives, the painful sex assessment was doing the work of listening to a person's Body for them. I was giving fish to hungry people. I needed to teach hungry people how to fish.

Approaching painful sex by focusing on and only using the "medical model" (medication, physical therapy, testing) doesn't ultimately work because after you have helped the body heal and feel better, you likely have not changed the person's story of sex. In many cases, you still haven't changed the original story. The message your Body was telling you in the first place.

In addition to working with your doctor, I would like to share with you some of the principles that are helpful in alleviating painful sex and the anxiety painful sex causes. Let's start with some things that your Body may want to tell you.

You aren't ready for sex.[18]

Sex isn't Intimacy.

Sex isn't automatically Pleasure.

Why are you having sex?[19]

Stop! You are too anxious, worried, tense, or confused about what is happening in the sexual encounter.[20]

Stop! Go see a doctor![21]

How to Get Past Painful Sex

Number One. There is no shortcut. You must attend to and listen to your Boat Body. You are the only one who can do it. Your doctor or your partner cannot do it for you. This includes understanding how to proactively desire and become aroused for sex.

Number Two. Many times, painful sex is caused by our stories or ideas of sex. Emphasis on "many." There are times when pain just happens, and it is the stories we begin to tell ourselves about the pain that hurt us and prolongs our struggle.

The Lubricant Stories. Lubricants are not a substitute for sexual arousal. Lubricants often mask understanding and sensing engorgement and readiness for penetration. For example, once the lubricant is applied, it is "go time," whether

---

18 It's not good to force your body to cooperate and respond to other people's arousal or need for sex.

19 If we have sex from a role, performance, or validation of self, we set ourselves up for the body to say, "No!"

20 For men, this is often a cause of erection and climax difficulties. For women, this is often the cause of Vaginismus, an involuntary tensing and tightening of the vaginal opening and vagina that causes burning, pain, and difficulty with penetration.

21 If you have pain, burning, dryness, cramping, and tightness more than a few times, you need a doctor's assessment and treatment. You might be experiencing an infection, hormonal imbalance, medications, nerve issues causing "hot spots"/painful spots, irregular structures of body (e.g., "tipped uterus" for women or for men "Peyronie's disease," which causes pain and irregularities in the shape of the penis).

the partner is ready or not. Another important issue with lubricant is that anything that is not the same pH of the vaginal tissues is likely to cause irritation. Any lubricant that has a preservative may cause irritation (and ultimately pain).

Erection Stories, as in Erection-Driven Sex. Same idea as above. Erections don't mean you are fully ready to have sex; for example, a wake-up-in-the-morning erection. Also, a partner may not automatically become aroused by seeing an erect penis.

"Enjoying Being Close" Stories. Frequently having penetration without arousal and climax, is a recipe for your vaginal tissues to chafe and become irritated. Your body is meant to send extra blood flow and lubricant to your genitalia with the arousal process. If you don't become aroused, it makes you vulnerable for your body to complain or to cause a breakdown of the tissues.

Trauma Stories. Your Body will remember and hold the story of traumatic events and situations that have harmed you. You must pay attention to your story. It is usually helpful to tell your story out loud to someone who is able to fully listen, understand your experience, and respond in a comforting way (trauma-informed therapist, wise partner, or friend). It is helpful to "work the hurt." "Work the hurt" is a phrase adapted from the phrase "Work the problem." It means that you are not powerless over the problem. You can find a way to move through your issue and your emotions to solve the problem. It is harmful to try to ignore or bury the triggers and hurt that come up when you approach intimacy and sexual activity. It is also likely that your Body won't let you. Be sure to recognize if you have had a traumatic experience even with a loving partner. You may need to address a pattern in your sex experiences with a long-term partner that your Body is trying to tell you about.

Number Three. Once you have a pain pattern (happening more than a few times) with arousal or penetrative intercourse, there is no getting away with "Closed Sex" experiences. The Closed Sex experiences, the 1, 2, 3, 4 plan, can keep you in an endless loop of "1-2-3 abort." Each interrupted sexual experience will make the body more determined to protect you. You can try, but each time pain is triggered, the pain may increase and happen sooner than the time before. If you don't listen to your Body, your Body has to shout.

So, what to do with painful sex?

You may have guessed it. We need to get to the better story and respond to the real experience of sex. We can add Pleasure to the experience. We ask "What if?" and then we find our What Is. We want to wake up in our Boat Body on our River Mind and paddle.

My most important task in helping people with painful sex, whether that is after a surgical procedure, or in the throes of chronic pain, is to help them wake up.

People who are awake listen to their Body's communications and they don't believe everything the River Mind pulls them into. Things like:

You are damaged goods. Something is wrong with you. You aren't a man anymore. You are broken. You are a failure.

These are stories that keep you focusing on the Outside you. They keep you trying hard not have pain. They are hurtful stories that make you want to curl up, go to sleep, and never think of sex again.

Become present to what your pain is telling you about your Body. Don't let your pain or your diagnosis sweep you away, tossing you over waterfalls of Mind and Body pain.

The way to move past painful sex is to "locate yourself" in your sexual activity. Remember to ask "What if?" my Body is telling me something important. Pay attention to the "What is?" of your 1, 2, 3, 4 list and begin to practice showing up.

To be clear, I don't know if you can get rid of your pain completely. I do know that becoming Responsive to your Self—moving your attention from your Outside self to your Inner Person Self during sex—is your best chance at moving beyond pain.

Painful sex is a mystery story, and the Body's actual experience gives us clues. I play detective and help the person's Body be heard. It's my job to figure out what the Body is saying and asking for.

No, disregard that.

It's my job to help my clients understand what their Body is communicating to them. What is your Body asking for?

It is likely that painful sex is inviting you to a different experience. The good part.

How to Show Up for Sex
Inner Person Self Sex

I think that by now, you are starting to notice there are some points that we keep revisiting. Each story of sexual problems, partnership distress, meltdowns, and self-doubt has ended with same moral to the story.

When life isn't going well, it's time to consider looking at what you don't know you don't know.

In regards to sex, it's time to look at the What Is—the better experience of the Inner Person Self during a sexual encounter.

Do you know how to wake up and be more present during sex?

At this point, you may be thinking what lots of clients have thought.

> *So, if my list of how to have sex isn't going to ultimately be that helpful, what in the world are you asking me to do?*

> *All this, "You are missing in sex." "You are asleep in your body boat on your mind river." And now you are saying that the four points to get to orgasm may actually cause sexual problems?*

> *I'm not sure I follow.*

> *Whoa, this stuff is way too theoretical, "teachey," and b-o-r-i-n-g! I am not sure how this is connected to helping sex get better.*

> *1, 2, 3, 4 works for me.*

I get it. It can be a lot.

And come to think of it, even if I don't like the How to Do Sex list, what else is there?

Fair enough! And I thought you'd never ask.

Currently you know the How to *Do* Sex graph, the straight line that crossed the threshold? You have an orgasm. Mission accomplished.

What if you changed the goal of sex?

What if your goal for having sex and doing sexual things was to experience full Mind, Body, and Inner Person Self presence? What if your intention was to embrace the whole painting? To feel grounded, centered, fully present? Content?

What if rather than achieving an orgasm, being satisfied, getting off, releasing tension, or having more than one orgasm—you focused on becoming fully present in the moment? This changes the experience from Did you go? Yes or no. Did you climax? Yes or no. And enables a different approach. Instead of "yes or no," what if we tried both? "Yes and yes."

What if your attention turned to "What is?" What if you watched the River Mind, scanned the Boat Body, and opened your Inner Person Self eyes? This would allow you to be in the present. You could be in your experience, not wrapped up in the story of the experience. Your being fully present in the moment would be an abutment to build a bridge. The kind of bridge that allows for connection to another Inner Person Self. Each Self could "walk" back and forth taking it all in. Two connected Selves who show up and practice Awakeness.

Were you present? Yes, and I had an orgasm. Both. Yes and yes. New goal. Presence while doing sexual things.

What if we drew a new graph? A graph that tracked our What Is wherever our experience took us?

Well, it just so happens that we do have that kind of a graph, that kind of a different arousal journey.

Showing Up for Sex

OPEN SEX EXPERIENCE

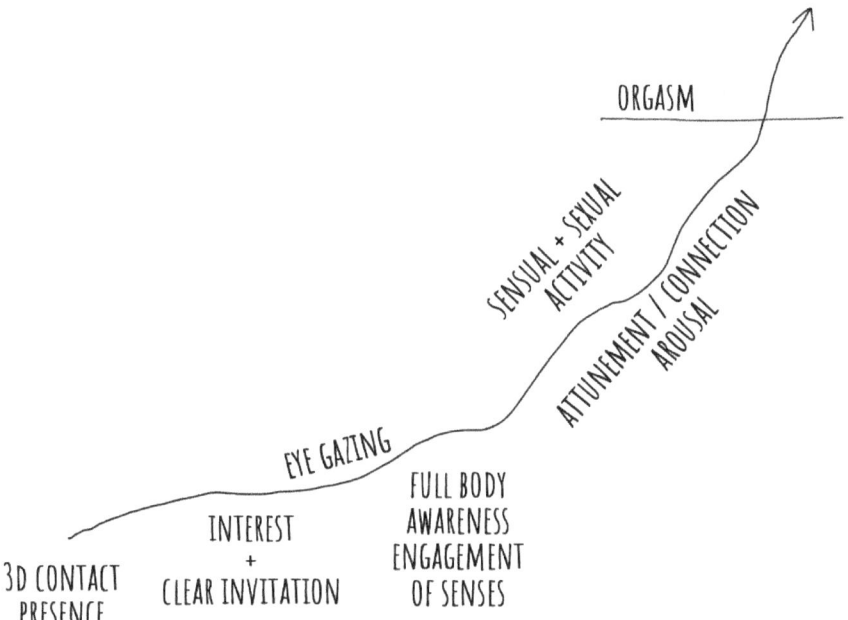

This graph shows what happens when you show up for sex. You leave the 1, 2, 3, 4 plan behind. It shows being Open (awake) and Responsive to the What Is. The up and down of the line shows the ebb and flow of arousal that doesn't bother you—doesn't cause anxiety that you won't get to orgasm, because orgasm is no longer the goal. The goal is to practice being present to the experience.

This is the Open Sex experience. It is how you go from approaching sex with your "Outside self," which is based on Roles, Performance, and Validation, to showing up with your awake and present Inner Person Self. Outside to Inside. Closed sexual experiences to Open sexual experiences.

Six ways to Show Up for Sex (Open Sex Experience)

Proactive Desire and Contact Connect with your partner before sex. Make an open connection, an Intimacy Bridge before you decide to have sex. Don't depend on a sexual encounter to create Intimacy.

Eye Gazing Despite what you usually do, or what you see in romantic scenes on TV or movies, open your eyes. Open your eyes and look into your partner's eyes. Eye-to-eye contact is a turbo-charged connection. When we look into someone's eyes we get emotional, mental, and physical information and we also send emotional, mental, and physical information. The eyes are the window to the Self. Not only does it mean you literally are awake, but the Inner Person Self is less likely to doze off if you are peering into another person's eyes. Eye-to-eye contact is such a powerful move because our Bodies will respond with oxytocin, a hormone that enhances our attention, focuses our awareness, and increases receptivity to contact.

Float/Become Present to the Moment Compare the 1, 2, 3, 4 plan for sex and the Show Up plan. The straight-up line means that once you are on Step 3, "doing sexual things," it's like you are on a train following tracks. Destination: orgasm. Anything that isn't part of the train track or gets in front of the train, may cause the train to derail. The stories that pop up in our River Minds are notorious for derailing us on our journey. "I'm not getting aroused, I can't climax, my partner is bored, this doesn't feel good," and on and on.

Instead of getting on the train tracks, follow the ebb and flow, the wide valleys and climbs of your arousal. Don't plan where the journey will take you, show up to take the journey. Don't push your arousal too quickly, just allow the arousal to come to you. If you notice that you don't seem to be aroused, let go of the bombardment of thoughts and stories from your River Mind and float. Let your thoughts float on by. Tune in to your "What is?"

Enjoyment/Pleasure (embodied joy, fun, play, body feel goods) In contrast to an arousal focus where our focus is on the line going up, we can show up for enjoyment and pleasurable feelings in our whole Body. We can feel our sexual arousal but not hurry it. Yes, arousal and Yes, Body Pleasure. Both. If we start to get distracted, we can return to focusing on what feels good for ourselves and our partner.

Sensuality (Engagement of the Body Senses and Sensations) The human body has numerous communication channels to give and receive information and energy. I often use the metaphor that a sense such as sight is like a USB port.

Our sight gives and gets information and energy. We also have sound, touch, taste, smell, movement/rhythm, Proprioception, Interception, and Vestibular.[22] Don't get caught on the train speeding to orgasm while the rest of your Body is sound asleep. Use and accentuate the sensation and pleasurable feelings of every part of your Body. Don't use the senses just for foreplay, but bring them into the whole process. Yes, Body Pleasure and Yes, arousal. Both.

Audible Feedback Loop If you are pretty quiet during sex and only make some noise when you are highly aroused and thrown into the pleasure of your orgasm, it is almost certain that you are fixated on your arousal and getting to climax. Same goes for dirty talk. If you want your partner to say naughty things to you because it turns you on, or you are trying to get your partner revved up, I think you are probably on the climax train. Now, of course, it isn't terrible if that is your plan and you enjoy it. But when things aren't working out during sex, you may want to reevaluate either too much silence or all the sexy talk. I do invite you to be noisy during sex. One reason you want to give sounds for feedback is because it is one of the ways we engage and wake up our whole Body. It is how you share your What Is experience with your partner. It is how you open your side of the Intimacy Bridge and invite your partner to do the same. It's a way to show up for sex together.

---

22 Proprioception (knowing where your body and parts of body are and controlling movement or stillness), Vestibular (sense of balance, coordination, and orientation to space), Interoception (awareness of internal bodily signals such as heart rate, hunger, tension in muscles, sexual energy, elimination).

Incompatible

The Back Door to Desire

Like so many of the couples I work with, the answer to Erica and Ted's sexual "incompatibility" wasn't to compromise.

Like, say, make Ted a little less interested in sex and Erica more interested. It wasn't going to work to get them to try new erotic things so they would find new stuff together. Erica had determined she wasn't interested. We were starting way far back from Step 1—Interest. Working to do the 1, 2, 3, 4 list better was a nonstarter.

And, anyway, it turns out that Pleasure was the key to opening the door to what they didn't know they didn't know. Pleasure is my go-to for helping people open their eyes in their Boat on their River.

It's surprising how powerful it is and how little thought a lot of us give it.

To be clear, I don't use the word "pleasure" to be a euphemism for sex. So what do I mean when I say Pleasure? Consider this definition. "Pleasure is a wake-up moment when we feel joy in our Body and Mind at the same time." Joy. Joy is energy. I love the word "enjoyment." Surrounded, immersed in joy.

One way to feel this Pleasure is to play and "enfun" yourself. Surround and immerse yourself in fun. Play and fun can only be experienced when you are in the present. You can say you will have fun in the future and you had fun in the past, but the experience of fun is an in-the-moment activity.

And what better way to have that happen but to laugh. A laugh is joy in the moment. Laughter is a Body Mind communiqué of joy.

If we think about the 1, 2, 3, 4 list we have been discussing about how to have sex, it is not clear that Pleasure is even a part of doing sex.

I know, I know. "Sex *is* fun." And it may well be. But I put it to you that if people don't like the sex they are having, it is not fun. To be fair, many people do call the activities of sex "sexual pleasure." I guess that could be a kind of fun.

319

Either way, whether doing sex is fun or not, Pleasurable or not, that doesn't help a couple if one person doesn't feel Pleasure and their partner is at wits' end to "pleasure" their partner.

It is not a given that doing sex provides arousal, orgasm, or Pleasure.

*   *   *

Ted, Erica, and I discuss Pleasure and how it might fit into their relationship. I ask Ted and Erica, "How do you experience Pleasure in your life?

Silence.

Ted speaks first. "Well, I have never used the word 'pleasure.' I have always thought of sex as pleasure. Yet I don't think I have ever had Pleasure with sex—at least not the kind you are talking about. Joy, in the moment, being connected to my body. My experience with sex is that the "pleasure" is what takes my mind and body to a trance-like space of ecstasy. That's what I like about it. I can leave the shit of life behind even if for a moment."

Erica joins in and speaks to Ted. "When I think of how long I've known you, I don't think of you as leaving room for fun. I mean you play with the kids, but even with that you aren't really all in. It's like you schedule twenty minutes for it, it's in your calendar, and you show up to spend quality time with the kids. I feel that way with sex as well. You have an idea of when we should have sex and when it is over, then it's on to the next thing.

"You don't do anything if it isn't measured or building for the future. Haven't I told you that you need friends, you need fun, or a hobby?" she adds.

Ted nods in agreement, but doesn't speak.

Erica then looks at me and says, "I don't use the words 'pleasure' or 'play' either. I do associate 'pleasure' as a way of saying sex, and I think of playing as what kids do. Tell me more about this joy idea."

I explain, "Joy is actually considered an emotion. And emotions are Body Mind communications to a person. An emotion is your Body's response to your experience. For example, joy or fun causes laughter. A timely cup of coffee causes you to take a deep, relaxing breath—an energetic change in the Body. Having fun gives you energy and a sense of ease (an energetic change in the Body) that makes effort easy and time pass without you noticing.

"To play, you come into the present moment. You focus on the What Is before you; it's a way of focusing, to stop thinking about anything but what you are playing at the moment."

I look at her. She had said in her email that she was quitting sex. Here comes an Aha! if she's ready.

"I think that you are at the beginning of learning to practice Pleasure in sex." She looks at me very skeptically.

I continue. "Well, you finally decided that if something didn't feel good you weren't going to keep doing it. You are tuning in to your Body."

Time to give Ted his Aha! "That's more than you are doing, Ted. You are using sex to get out of your Body and go to another place. And, most important-ly, you two are not at all skilled at enjoying Pleasure together."

After checking that the messages hit their mark and didn't come on too strong, we discuss their homework assignment.

"Go home and think about it. Do some research. Each of you, individually, find something you enjoy and try it. The goal is to see if you can feel Pleasure. Not sexual pleasure, but the Pleasure of being alive, Pleasure in your body, or something that brings you joy or laughter."

Graduation

Contented.

It is ten months later.

Erica and Ted sit in the faded lemon-yellow leather chairs in my office.

I feel expectantly excited. It seems like today will be graduation. I will say my goodbyes to them with the offer of returning at any time, and maybe a checkup session in six months if they want it.

They are recently back from a second honeymoon trip and the news is delightful.

Unlike their first honeymoon, they have been in a love, sex, and connection heaven. They are peaceful and relaxed.

Their sex therapy journey wasn't what they expected and it wasn't easy. They had not restarted their sex life because I showed them amazing sex secrets and showed them some high-quality sex toys, educational videos with sexual techniques, and breathing exercises.

No, my part was helping them see what was missing in their ideas of sex and sexual experiences. They were missing. They "knew" how to do sex, but they didn't know how to show up and experience sex.

Erica started the ball rolling by deciding that sex didn't feel good, that she didn't like sex. So much so that she decided to quit sex.

I listened to her story of sex. She was having sex because that was her role as a partner (Latent Self). She needed to have sex (Performance Self) because her husband felt loved and desirable that way (Validation Self).

As so often happens, Erica, who supposedly wasn't very sexual, was further along in her understanding of her sexual self than Ted.

Although Ted thought that he was more sexual than his wife—he wanted more sex, he thought about sex more—he was still approaching sex by doing sex.

His story of sex was that he needed to feel desired and loved. The couple's Intimacy Bridge was closed. Their Inner Person Selves were deeply asleep during sex.

The journey from an email with a plea for help to a whole new sex life that they both felt good about was a lot of work. The couple worked on talking and understanding each other and moving forward together with their real experiences. They practiced many, many Knee-to-Knee Exercises, and from there moved to the "Proactive Desire" exercises of the Yellow Light Encounters.[23]

Partnership, Intimacy, Sexuality, Pleasure, Sex, and Erotic Flow were all on the table to understand and experience.

Our sessions and the couple's discussions at home were filled with Boat, River, Person topics and the stories of sexuality that came to light. We looked at their partnership. They already had good partnership skills in most of their life, until it came to partnering in sex.

The couple took the Sexual Experience and Behavior Inventory (SEABI), which allowed them to compare their template stories about sex.

The couple practiced Intimacy Bridge conversations, and became skillful at the I Count–You Count Dialog.

We worked with the whiteboard to plot and understand the arousal pathway that the couple used.

"Change the goal," "Don't have sex, show up for sex," "Don't focus inward, focus on the present."

We delved into how to practice Erotic Flow that happens when you open an Intimacy Bridge and stay with both yourself and your partner in the moment.

The couple listened, discussed, argued, and kept practicing those Knee-to-Knees.

The turning point Aha! breakthrough took its time in coming, but it finally arrived.

For this couple, it was the Pleasure piece, the idea of embodied joy, that helped them wake up. More specifically, wrestling. It was wrestling that took them to a place they didn't know they didn't know. Once there, they would never return to the distress of incompatibility.

After the couple shared that they didn't really use or think of the word "pleasure," and in Ted's case he didn't think he really "did" pleasure, I assigned them to find something they experienced Pleasure with.

---

23 See a description of the Yellow Light Encounters Exercise in the Appendices.

It took a couple of sessions, but it was Ted who got the action moving on this one. He came back and gave a report.

"I found a pleasurable moment. It was with Coco, our dog. What happened was I was sitting on the couch and throwing the ball down the hall for her to fetch. She loves to get that ball and bring it back to me. This time, I threw it so hard that it bounced back and rolled under the sectional and stayed there.

"I got up and got on my hands and knees and had to lay flat on my stomach to stretch and reach the ball. Coco lunged excitedly, poking her nose under the couch and then licking my ear and then nose back under the couch; she was leaning and rolling all of her weight onto me. Doing her excited little yip, poking her nose under the couch, licking my ear in rapid frenetic movements. She flailed her legs out and again threw her weight on my back. It was so comical.

"I began to laugh so hard that I could hardly get the ball out.

"There she was slobbering, licking, and trembling with excited energy about me getting the ball for her. It hit me. This was pleasure. Her joy was in her mind and in her body. My joy was in my mind when I saw her so excited and goofy. It made me laugh uncontrollably. Harder than I have laughed in a long time. It felt good.

"Even though I never thought about pleasure, and for sure got worried when you talked about it that first time, I knew that this was pleasure.

"Fast Forward to our Yellow Light Encounters. The handbook had exercises in it to help us build an Intimacy Bridge. I saw the wrestling one, and thought about that day I had stretched out on the floor and laughed at Coco. The next time it was my turn, I invited Erica to a wrestling match."

Erica now chimes in.

"I was very surprised he wanted to do this. We tried and soon we were laughing a lot. It was ludicrous. Two adults rolling around on the floor in a free-for-all to pin someone's arm down for seven seconds. We have not laughed that hard and that long together ever!

"After we exhausted ourselves, we were just there together on the floor quietly looking into each other's eyes. It wasn't awkward at all."

Erica and Ted continued to practice being present with each other and they moved on to other planned and deliberate experiences of emotional, mental, and physical contact. The Yellow Light Encounters had become something they looked forward to.

Erica remarked several times, "I love this. I've never seen Ted so present and paying attention to me and to what we do together."

Along the way, Erica began noticing something else. She shared this in a session.

"I began to think about our sex therapy, how you really had never told me that I had to like sex, or even asked me to try to find something to turn me on or try sexually. I had expected that you would, since you are a sex therapist.

"And I thought about Ted. I could tell he was not faking just to get to the sex part. He was really into the exercises. Which surprised me. He's not one to follow the rules or use language that he thinks is imprecise, childish, or silly. Yet, each and every time he showed up.

"In addition to noticing an attitude change in him, I began to notice how I enjoyed the stuff we were practicing. Being held. The exercises to touch like a starfish or using the triangle touch.

"But most surprising to me was from the very first time when Ted said, 'We are going to wrestle!' and we got down on the floor and wrestled, I felt a new sexual zing. I felt it and I pictured having sex with Ted and it made me laugh more.

"I did not share this with Ted right away. I wanted to make sure I was sure. I had really, really meant it that I was done with sex.

"Once I told Ted about my new interest in sex, I had another surprise. He didn't immediately want to have sex. He never said a word about it. We didn't talk about it. He continued to take his turn on our Yellow Lights, I continued to take my turn.

It was only in a session with you, Dr. Lisa, when you brought it up. You asked, 'Do you want to see if you like sex now?' that the topic was opened back up.

"And as you know, we did start sex again. We used the wrestling exercises, and we used the 'I'm green light. Are you green light?' words to invite each other to sex. It didn't sound awkward or canned like I worried it would. Not at all. It felt just right. It flowed. There was no worry, mixed messages, or hesitation for either of us."

Ted adds, "Our sex life is completely different. I never imagined how it could be. Now that we are doing sex together, I feel a new sense of peace inside."

Erica smiles and nods in agreement.

Ted and Erica crossed over to understand and be Responsive to their Inner Person Self. Becoming Responsive enabled them to have experiences together that included both Selves. Both Inner Person Selves were awake and included. Previously, their sex life had been based on the roles of the Latent, Performance, and Validation. Through a seemingly bad turn in their sex life, they had learned to become Responsive to Self. They had integrated their Inner Person Selves into their sexual experiences. The good part.

By learning to be awake and present in their Boat on their River, they were able to show up and include their whole self in their sexual experiences.

They took the Outside-In journey to Awakeness and found a new sex life.

This is a story of sex and it isn't a story of sex.

Yes, and yes.

Both.

Appendices

Concept Guide
About the Word "Practice"
Wake-Up Opportunities
Knee to Knee (K2K) Practice
First Aid for Anxiety and Depression
Breath
Wake-Up Practice
Grief and Crisis
Body Awakeness Ideas
Journeys to Awakeness
Sexual Arousal Pathways
Stages of Awakeness
I Count—You Count Agreement
About the Yellow Light Encounter Practice
About the Sexual Experiences and Behavior Inventory (SEABI)

Concept Guide

Here are the working definitions of important concepts in this book. They have been capitalized throughout the text.

Awakeness A state of being awake and fully aware in the present moment—alive, aliveness. An understanding of Self that helps you focus your attention to the aliveness of the present moment. The practice of thinking about thinking, thinking less, being aware of your whole Body, and noticing the present through the sensory inputs of the Body.

Boat Body A phrase from the "Boat. River. Person." metaphor to represent and describe the dynamic human body and its ability to access and interact with the world, remember, experience the world, and communicate with both the person's Mind and the Person Self living in the Body.

Contentment A feeling of peace and assuredness that you are okay, lovable, worthy, and desirable that releases you from the need to strive or control your experiences or search for a sense of Self from outside sources. Contentment with Self.

Erotic Flow A state of Awakeness during sexual arousal and activity. Thoughts and a sense of time are suspended or lessened and a rich and pervasive sense of clarity, being alive, energized, and whole is common.

Equal Say So refers to the partnership agreement of the "I Count—You Count" commitment which is illustrated by a graph. The graph depicts a line between two lists that represents two people in partnership who attend and advocate for "their side of the line" while at the same time honor, work to understand, and validate "their partner's side of the line." Both sides of the line count equally.

I Count–You Count is a value statement that describes an "Equal Say So partnership." The I Count–You Count principle is depicted in a graph with two lists containing Thoughts, Emotions, Needs, Wants/ Desires, Fears, "personal stuff," Body messages, Body energy, and Body sensations. In partnership, both sides of the line are explored in order to honor each side and provide an equality of power. This is a framework for a respectful, functioning partnership that enables breaking emotional gridlock and respectful problem solving.

Inner Self The inside, conscious space of a human person that is aware of and works to understand thoughts, sensations, energy and concepts that are present in the Mind and Body. Most importantly it is where each person actually lives and is alive. When we pay attention to our Mind and Body and respond based on the information they are giving us, we are awake.

Inner Person Self A phrase from the "Boat. River. Person." metaphor to represent and describe a human's Self. We often don't realize that we have not taken up our personal power to guide our lives wisely. Our Inner Person Self is the most precious, capable, and wise thing we have as humans. And as far as anyone knows, we only get one.

Intimacy The skill and practice of experiencing another person while staying present to your own experience.

Intimacy Bridge A metaphor to describe a state of mutual Awakeness when two people are engaging in conversation, mutual understanding, physical touch, and presence.

Outer/Outside Self Our view of our Self based on our environment. The outside environment of a human person impacts, influences, and changes the human person. We start our lives by identifying who we are and what we are about and how we are doing based on our environment, comparison to and feedback from others.

Partnership "Equal Say So" functioning and behaviors.

Pleasure A message from your Body that spontaneously says, "Joy!" Embodied Joy and "feel goods."

Process Therapy A therapist-led conversation that practices using the I Count–You Count agreement, attending to your side of the line, your partner's side of the line, and Awakeness. Helpful to practice waking up and dissolving emotional gridlock.

River Mind A phrase to describe and represent our thoughts and stream of consciousness. The Mind is like a river, always flowing. The Mind is the most influenced by other people and the Outside environment. Most of us think that this River is our Self. If we are floating wherever our Minds take us, we, our Inner Person Selves, are asleep. Try raising your attention above the River of thoughts. Watch the River move past you.

Self "Self" capitalized represents your true Inner Person Self. The word "self" without the capital represents a general reference to you or your Outside Self.

Sexuality A person's Sexuality is like a scrapbook where they have collected stories about Self, sex, and identity. Each story that is clipped and pasted into the book, especially the ones that a person keeps turning to and remembering, is a story about Self. Each story tells whether you are awake in your Boat and your River.

Put another way, are the stories in your book about Performance or about Responsiveness? When you are engaged in sex, do you strive for climax or do you strive to be fully present and in the moment to the What is of the experience?

What do the stories from your book tell you about how you see yourself with sex and gender? What do your stories of who or what attracts you reveal about your Responsiveness to Self? When you look at your sense of who you are sexually, do you feel at home in your body, at peace, awake, and alive? Or do you feel scattered, anxious, stressed, like you can't rest or that something is wrong with you?

Views of Self Five stages/levels of how we understand our Self: Latent Self, Performance Self, Validation Self, Responsive Self, Integrated Self.

What if? A question that the Inner Person Self asks of the Mind and the Body in order to be wise about a problem.

What is? A question from the Inner Person Self to focus attention to the present moment—Awakeness assisted by Mind (River) and Body (Boat).

What Is A state of being fully aware and present to the reality of the moment. Awakeness.

About the Word "Practice"

There are lots of suggestions in this book about taking action. Ask "What if?" Ask "What is?" Wake up. Find your Self. Be Responsive to your Inner Person Self. Include your Self. Integrate your Self into your whole life. Find Contentment.

While these goals give us a direction to aim for, not one of us will finally arrive to always be "Awake," wise, and Content. I suggest using the word "practice" to think and speak about the principles of Outside Self and Inner Person Self.

Keisha Bush[24] notes that the distinction from being to practicing is a more realistic, honest, and sustainable goal.

She shares four reasons why using the word "practice" (e.g., "I practice Waking up," "I practice Contentment") is helpful:

- Practice is a form of action.
- Practice infers that I can always improve.
- To practice is to say there is no endpoint to the activity that I am practicing.
- To practice is to include rest, as no one can be active nonstop without pause.

---

24 Keisha Bush is the author of *No Heaven for Good Boys*. She wrote an inspiring article in the March 2023 issue of the magazine *Lion's Roar* called "How to Not Burn Out." In it, she advises that it is better to use the word "practice" rather than put a label or a title on ourselves (e.g., I am Awake, I am Integrated, I am Contented).

Wake Up Opportunities

There are numerous situations that provide opportunities to focus on and practice waking up and being present:

Exercise, walking, sports, dance.

Body exertion and movement.

Activities that require you to have physical rhythm with other people. Manual labor, building, group dance, timed and scheduled activity.

Sexual arousal and sexual encounters.

Go to places with "big air." Wide-open spaces. A very large building, A prairie. Stand in the midst of skyscrapers. Being outdoors in open air or in nature. The feeling of space that open air affords, gives us some room to put some white space around our thoughts.

Being outdoors or in an organic or natural environment. Observing nature and the natural world invites us to witness and observe the idea and energy of life. How does a boulder that seems to have no life of itself connect with all living things? What energy does the weather immerse you in? How do colors or smells impact your now or your What Is experience?

Quiet times and spaces.

Focusing on any kind of beauty (order, rhythm) or anti-beauty (disorder, chaos) wherever you find it (e.g. the mundane, art, music).

Pleasure. The wake-up definition of pleasure is embodied joy. That means you feel your body responding to something positively—often spontaneously. Laughing, clapping, sighing, letting out a deep breath to relax, singing, whistling.

Conversations with others, especially with people who practice I Count–You Count attitudes and behaviors.

Activities with others, especially those with a common goal.

Having prolonged close proximity with other people.

Engaging in, being curious about, immersing yourself in another person's world.

Reflecting on and sharing a complete picture of your personal life and world with safe and willing others. Consider asking others about their complete picture.

"Work the hurt." When you have a painful or uncomfortable experience, turn toward the experience, not away. Start with your What Is. Next, identify an emotion word that resonates with you. Next, find the lesson or the wisdom you can glean from the clarity of naming and describing your experience.

Life milestones.

Birth, death, illness.

Birthdays, graduations, reunions, weddings.

Divorce, break-ups, separations.

New job, leaving job, loss of job, retirement.

Moving, traveling.

Family gatherings.

Friendships, new relationships.

Crisis.

Knee-to-Knee Practice (K2K)

K2K Practice Overview

Time needed to complete the exercise: three to five minutes.

This exercise is an opportunity to practice presence together (Integration) as a couple. The goal is to create space and time to practice the habit of proactively making time for connection, inviting your partner to a 3D connection, and experiencing awake and present connection with your partner. We also can use the idea of building an Intimacy Bridge, or making bids for contact.

Partners take turns inviting and leading the exercise within a time window of every forty-eight hours to seventy-two hours. That means they can invite the very first hour or the last hour. (Although waiting until the very last hour every time could send the wrong message.) Partners should choose the optimal length of the window for the exercise ahead of time.

The leader invites their partner to the exercise using words that express desire for connection.

The leader arranges furniture and takes the lead in setting up for the K2K, and approaches their partner to verbally invite to the activity. The leader invites their partner using inviting and positive requests (e.g., "I would like to do our K2K with you now, is it a good time?"). The leader should attend to their timing to make it easy for a partner to respond positively.

To the partner who has been invited, take care to answer in a positive manner (e.g., "Yes, give me five minutes." And then be sure to be ready in five minutes). Avoid declining. If you decline the invitation, it is an immediate rain check and you are now the leader.

Sit in comfortable chairs. Face each other directly, touch knees, and hold hands. Maintain eye contact. Ask your partner to share their emotional high and low of the day (week, trip, experience). Then, briefly acknowledge and empathize with your partner's experience and response. Then switch roles.

You can use different words to inquire about the emotional high and emotional low. "What made you happiest today? What was most disappointing about your day?"

The goal of this exercise is not to get a long discussion started, although it is okay to continue talking. It is also okay to use a short acknowledgment to what your partner shares, e.g., "I would be upset about that too!" "That's fantastic!" "Thank you for sharing the emotions of your day with me." A guideline is that the sharing partner shares about a paragraph and the listener responds with a sentence or two.

The three dimensions (3D) of contact we focus on are Emotional, Mental, and Physical.

The Emotional Connection Part

Asking and sharing events that have emotional energy. "Extra points" if you actually label and use emotion/feeling words, e.g., I felt flattered, proud, rejected, embarrassed.

Observing and attuning to your own and your partner's emotional energy.

The Mental Connection Part

Desire for connection is translated into a commitment to and follow-through to practice the exercise.

Honoring the commitment to take your turn as leader sends the meaning message to your partner that they and your relationship are important to them. This acts out, affirms what the relationship means for you.

Attentiveness to what your partner is sharing and willingness to share builds emotional and reassuring trust.

In addition, sharing specific events gives a partner more information and insights into their partner's day to day life.

The exercise is practicing "proactive desire." The commitment to doing the exercise is a shared meaning and the follow-through is an affirmation of the meaning.

The Physical Connection Part

Eye contact and gazing allows for physical presence, focus in the moment, and attunement with your partner.

Knees touching and holding hands is physical contact. Adhering to this posture allows a couple to practice reaching out to make and receive proactive physical contact.

Physical connection also is expressed by being fully present and in the moment (paying attention to what's happening and what you and your partner are experiencing in the moment).

K2K is not a "how was your day?" ritual. It is a deliberate effort for two people to attune to each other's emotions, thoughts, meanings, presence, and body energy.

The K2K is not practicing foreplay for sex.

It is important to consider how you respond when your partner invites you. If you are in the midst of something, let them know how long you need and then follow through promptly. Remember you are practicing your meanings. If you are not able to say yes to an invitation, you should call a raincheck. A raincheck means that you are instantly the leader and have forty-eight hours-seventy-two hours to invite and lead out in K2K.

If you or your partner travel and are absent, you can suspend the forty-eight hours or do a phone/virtual K2K check-in. Some couples prefer to do their K2K check-ins on the weekends or days off due to shared child care, shift constraints, or travel. The important part is you decide together and you treat it as an important commitment.

It is important that the leader is the partner who keeps track of the forty-eight hours. If it is not your turn, do not remind your partner. If your partner does not invite when it is their turn, wait a day or two and then speak with them. Reevaluate both of your commitments to the exercise. If you have a hard time keeping track of your forty-eight hours, use your phone or calendar to remind you. Another technique that many couples have found success with is to get an object, a magnet, a picture, or a sign and move it to their desk, their sink, their side of the bed when it is their turn.

The K2K connection encourages each partner, each Person in the Boat on their River, to wake up.

First Aid for Anxiety and Depression

First Aid for Anxiety and Depression

If your inner world is chaotic, with lots of thoughts popping in and out, it is likely your River Mind is focused on the possible stories of the future (anxiety, worry).

If your inner world is heavy, with lots of repeated thoughts (merry-go-round thoughts), it is likely you are focused on the past. Your Boat has been caught up in the whirlpool of the River and you are going round and round (depression, sadness).

Direct the beam of your attention somewhere else:

- Walk. You don't have to walk far, and you don't have to go fast, walk for exercise, or walk to get somewhere. Simply go outside and walk at an easy pace or even a slow pace.
- Recite affirmations that focus on the present moment, e.g., "Life happens in the now" or "I am breathing and I am okay right this minute."
- Gratitude. Pick five things you are grateful for right now, this minute. It does not matter if it is something large or very small, e.g., "I am grateful for the silence of this moment. I am grateful that I feel rested. I am grateful that I will have time to take a nap. I am grateful for the sunshine. I am grateful that I will get to see my friend tomorrow."
- Read. Preferably not something on the internet unless your device is offline. Feed your mind uplifting, supportive, interesting thoughts and ideas that have nothing to do with you and your life today, or have everything to do with what you are experiencing.
- Talk to another person or animal.
- Practice the Wake-Up Exercise.
- Focus on your breathing. Do a breath exercise.
- Use "Thought Stopping." Visualize a stop sign. Say, "Stop" out loud. Think of something beautiful, happy, soothing to turn your attention to and to

focus on. Think of directing the spotlight of your attention to something more positive.

- Do stream of consciousness writing on a piece of paper or journal. For most people this will be most effective to write by hand instead of typing. It might also be helpful to make a voice recording of your stream of consciousness conversation.

Breath

Basic Breath Connection

At any time and in any place, you always have the most basic way to focus on your breath. Here's how:

Tune in to your breath. Take a breath and say silently in your mind, "In." Breathe out all the air you can while thinking, "Out." Repeat. With each breath, try to make each In and Out slightly longer than the last breath. Just one breath that you tune in to and label will make a difference in how you feel.

Box Breathing

Box Breathing is a wonderful exercise that uses the mental picture of a box to help you tune in to your breath. You start by breathing in for three counts. That means you say 1, 2, 3 in your mind while taking in air. Then you hold that breath while you count to 1, 2, 3. Then you exhale, let out the breath, while you again count to 1, 2, 3. Lastly, keeping your lungs empty, don't breathe in for the count of 1, 2, 3. And then start "going around the four sides of the box" again.

Choose any number between 1-7 that works for you.

Wake-Up Practice

Basic What Is Practice to Wake Up and Be Present

Start with your breath. Focus on your breathing. Take a deep inhale and release.

Scan your body for sensations and energy levels.

Notice everything you can all around you using your senses (sight, smell, taste, touch, sound, rhythms). It may be helpful to name what you notice either in your mind or out loud. If you are feeling really distracted, you may want to write them down.

Direct your attention to your thoughts. Think about thinking. If you think of your thoughts as a river, do not get in the river, but rather watch the water thoughts go by. Notice what thoughts are doing to your body. Don't try "not to think." Rather think of a plane flying in the sky—don't concentrate on the plane but think about the sky around the plane. You can notice the plane flying through the sky, but your focus is on wider picture of the sky.

Another method is when you have a thought, visualize the word or the sentence and focus on the white space between the letters and the lines of words.

Periodically come back to your breath.

Bring your inner world to calm and quiet by cycling through these steps.

Grief and Crisis

Grief and Crisis

If you have intense pain and distress, it's helpful to have first aid–like ideas about how to "Self-Soothe" and get through the experience. Here are three principles to navigate through tough times.

First, do not ask "Why me?" or "What did I do to deserve this?" Instead, remember that this is the human experience. Being alive always leaves us open to pain, suffering, loss, distress, and disaster. No human truly escapes the reality of "What Is." There is no perfect life, getting life just right, or perfect people.

Second, be proactive in where you allow your River Mind—your attention—to focus. Don't allow your distress to take over your ability to tune in to the good, the beautiful, the comforting. Focus on, amplify the smallest relief, the smallest beauty, the smallest joy, the smallest grateful feeling, the smallest comfort of day-to-day routine.

One idea is to take a time out from thinking about your pain. Two minutes, ten, or thirty. Focus on something—a fond memory, something beautiful, or just resting.

Another idea is to label your experience. Find the exact words that describe your experience and resonate with you, e.g., embarrassed, ashamed, devastated, mortified, terrified, heavy dread, my heart hurts, I can't breathe, I am stunned, I can't speak. I can't think.

Once you have a word or words that match what your experience is, say the words (either out loud or in your mind). As you focus on your word, your experience, keep the word in mind as you take a deep breath in. Hold your breath a couple of beats, and then release, allowing the air to flow out of your lungs. As the air leaves think of your pain being carried out with it. Pause a couple of beats. Pain in. Pain out. Repeat until you feel an easing of the pain or discomfort.[25]

Third, ask yourself "Is this serving me?" or, another way to say it, "Is this helping me or hurting me?" Don't allow any one situation, loss, devastation, person or event to rob you of your responsibility and privilege to fully live your

25 I first heard of and adapted this exercise from Pema Chodron's writings. It can be found in her book *Welcoming the Unwelcome: Wholehearted Living in a Brokenhearted World.*

life. It's up to you to find peace and solace, "self-soothe," put up a boundary, move away from, stop things that are hurting you. It is a privilege to steer and live your life no matter what you encounter.[26]

Choose to live the life you have; you have no other options.

---

26 These principles were from Lucy Hone, a Resiliency expert in a TEDx Talk on September 25, 2019. The specific suggestions of what to do are largely from my work and experiences.

Body Awakeness Ideas

Our wise and wondrous Boat Body is an important part of being awake and assists us in practicing wholeness, presence, and Contentment. When we pay attention to our bodies and what messages the body gives us, we access valuable information that gives us wisdom in our day-to-day life.

Another way to think of Body Awakeness is to use the word "embodiment." Embodiment means awareness of and including your body. It means you take your body wherever you go and you let it guide you. You know its wisdom and know its language and you listen to it. Pay close attention to its wisdom.

Ideas for how to become more Body Awake

Pay attention to Body Sensations. Sensations are the language of the Body. Pain, discomfort, relaxed, neutral, numb, pleasure, hunger, cold, hot, new/novel sensations (e.g., how your body feels after an intense workout that you pushed into your limits, taking an ice bath, ice cubes, hot wax, slaps, yoga binds, compression sensations, constraint from ropes or spatial play, roller coaster, flying). Energy levels and shifts of energy (e.g., relaxed, antsy, energy crash, energy boost, release, excitement, sexual arousal, heaviness, depression). Specific areas and body parts: exterior body (e.g., skin sensations such as itches, tickling, burning, dryness), interior body (e.g., heart rate, hunger, nausea, elimination, muscle tension), balance and body position awareness (e.g., ability to coordinate movement, stillness, movement preciseness, movement memory, know where your body or a body part is without seeing it).

Notice Pleasure and Enjoyment. Pleasure comes directly and spontaneously from the Body. Laughing, clapping, sighing, letting out a deep breath to relax, sighing, whistling, listening to music, singing.

Notice Dread and Discomfort. A message to take notice of and understand. When we experience dread or uneasiness we can decide if we will push through or let it guide us in our response. Signs of Dread or Discomfort: Unusually sleepy; tired; low energy and motivation; heaviness in body; difficulty resting, relaxing, or sleeping; zoning out, detachment, numbness.

Movement: Move! Exercise, walking, chores, swim, sports, manual labor, dancing to music or without music, being in a crowd, moving against the flow of a crowd, moving with the flow of a crowd, spontaneous vocalizations and movement such as in a concert or at a sports event, holding purposefully still, rhythmic movement, free form movement to music, singing (projection and guiding your voice), and playing a musical instrument.

More Ideas: to help you focus in on your Body:

"The joy is in the journey." Seeing and experiencing the sights along the way.

"Body Scan." Assess all of your body for body sensations, energy levels, pleasure and enjoyment, or dread and discomfort.

"What is?" assessment: Check your thoughts. Assess your body. Notice your immediate surroundings with all of your senses. Stay focused in the moment; shut down future thinking or past thinking by focusing on your "in breath" and your "out breath."

Journeys to Awakeness

Journeys to Awakeness

Sleeping, Sleepy

Latent Self

IS UNDERSTOOD THROUGH ROLES AND THE CONTEXT AND CULTURE OF YOUR LIFE AND ORIGINS

Performance Self

IS UNDERSTOOD THROUGH EXPECTATIONS, VALUES, COMPARISON

Validation Self

IS UNDERSTOOD BY OTHER'S REACTIONS

Understand Self from OUTSIDE

Understand Self from INSIDE

Awakening, Awake

Responsive Self

IS UNDERSTOOD THROUGH PERSONAL EXPERIENCE AND PRESENCE

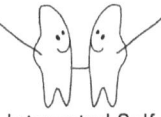

Integrated Self

IS BROUGHT/INCLUDED INTO THE PRESENT AND INTO INTERACTIONS WITH OTHERS. I COUNT – YOU COUNT RELATIONSHIPS. SPACIOUS ROOM FOR ALL (BOTH) 'SELF'S'

Sexual Arousal Pathways

Sexual Arousal Pathway

Closed vs. Open

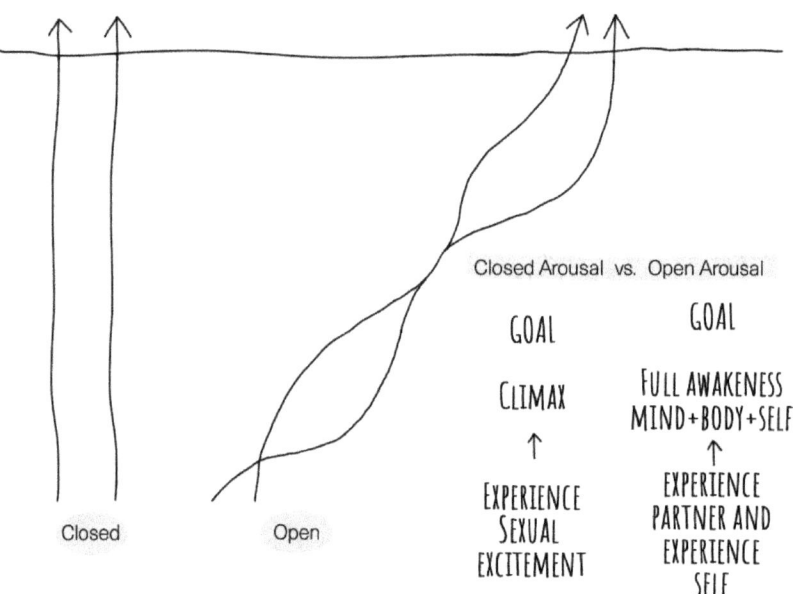

Closed Arousal vs. Open Arousal

GOAL

GOAL

CLIMAX

FULL AWAKENESS
MIND+BODY+SELF

↑

↑

EXPERIENCE
SEXUAL
EXCITEMENT

EXPERIENCE
PARTNER AND
EXPERIENCE
SELF

Closed

Open

Stages of Awakeness

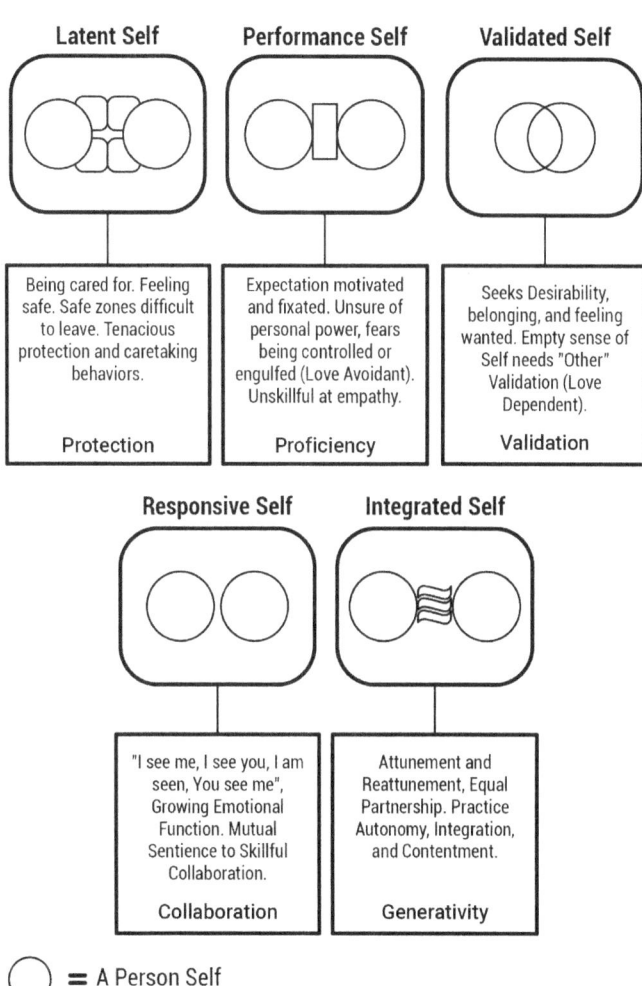

STAGES OF AWAKENESS

Latent Self	Performance Self	Validated Self
Being cared for. Feeling safe. Safe zones difficult to leave. Tenacious protection and caretaking behaviors.	Expectation motivated and fixated. Unsure of personal power, fears being controlled or engulfed (Love Avoidant). Unskillful at empathy.	Seeks Desirability, belonging, and feeling wanted. Empty sense of Self needs "Other" Validation (Love Dependent).
Protection	Proficiency	Validation

Responsive Self	Integrated Self
"I see me, I see you, I am seen, You see me", Growing Emotional Function. Mutual Sentience to Skillful Collaboration.	Attunement and Reattunement, Equal Partnership. Practice Autonomy, Integration, and Contentment.
Collaboration	Generativity

◯ = A Person Self

I Count–You Count Agreement

The I Count–You Count Agreement is a framework that helps couples practice more effective partnership in their day-to-day life and relationship. It can be used for easing and avoiding emotional and mental gridlock and practicing functioning relationship skills that provide Contentment. The skills of I Count–You Count enable each partner the agency (power) to impact the relationship, feel heard, honored, and Content. The I Count–You Count Grid is a visual illustration and tool to assist in practice of the agreement.

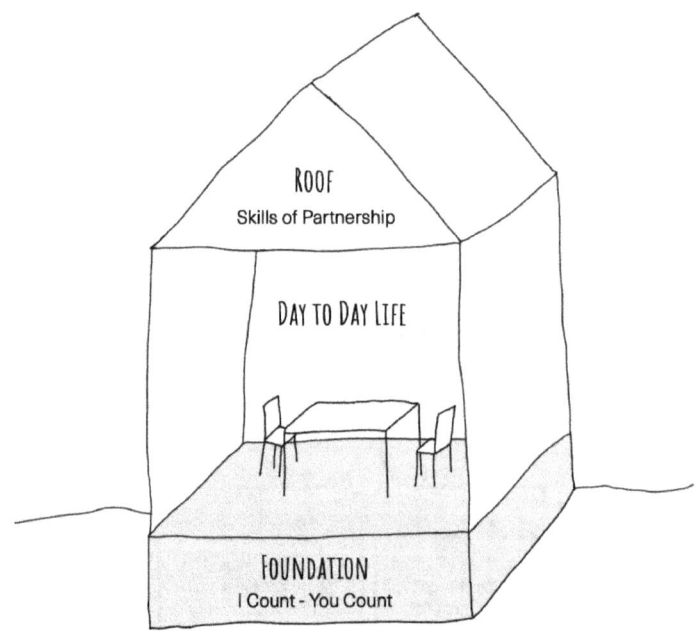

Step One Think, study, discover, get clear, name, and own your side of the line—your truth, your experience. Use the I Count–You Count grid that follows

Step Two Talk (either partner can start). Tell your partner about your side of the line, and keep advocating for your side of the line even if it is difficult. Ask your partner to talk about their side of the line, and keep asking questions until you thoroughly understand their side of the line. Keep trying to fully understand your partner's side of the line even if it is challenging (you don't agree on the premise, you think they are wrong, etc.).

Step Three Problem Solve for both sides of the line—work to change the problem. Talk (adjust your side of the line as needed, research, experiment, make commitments and agreements) to get to a Win-Win. A Win-Win is a resolution that honors, acknowledges, and/or takes into account both sides of the line. This may be a long process, and may be considered "a work in progress" for a lengthy time.

The power of a partnership is in the keeping of the foundation (I Count–You Count) strong.

You can change or repair the roof of partnership skills (awareness, communication, problem solving), and your house can be remodeled to look different (day-to-day life), but as long as you have the foundation in place, the house (the ability to interact in an effective way) will stand.

Guidelines

Win-Win and Imbalances

Truly split down the middle, an "equal operating partnership" does not happen all that often in real life. The "House of our Relationship" may have imbalances, sometime quite large inequalities.

The way to tell if it is an imbalance that should be worked on is if it causes a partner discomfort or pain. If your partner tells you something that doesn't feel good, rational, or correct to you, you still believe them (if it is an I Count–You Count relationship).

Examples of factors that could be very unbalancing to the relationship:

- A partner's job or career (lots of hours worked per week, travel, large difference in income earned).
- A partner's chronic or lengthy illness (physical, mental, or emotional debilitation).
- A partner who is "otherly abled" (known or undiscovered), e.g., physical disability, Neurodivergent, Autistic, PTSD, Dementia, Trauma.
- A partner in crisis, e.g., extended family issues, addictions, legal issues, illegal activity, mental illness.
- A partner who has an affair, infidelity, betrays (known or undiscovered).

- A partner who is not truthful (omits, spins, or withholds information), has power secrets or lies.
- A partner who does not, will not, is unable to let your side of the line count, e.g., patterns of unresolved aggression, withholding information, commitment, affection, time, resources, or attention.

If there is a consistent imbalance or a power secret, it is important to establish the foundation of I Count–You Count before working on a resolution or a game plan for the unbalancing issue. It is unlikely that an issue can be resolved to Contentment (healthy relationship) if one partner consistently "Counts" more than their partner.

Win-Win

Equal partnership does not mean that everything is equal. It means that each partner and their side of the line is equally valued and honored. A Win-Win may be an imbalanced situation that the couple is aware of and implements practices to assist with the imbalance so that it does not unduly burden one of the partners. Sometimes the Win is just to be heard and your side of the line acknowledged. Sometimes the Win would be giving your partner the gift of allowing the imbalance without strings while being sure to honor how you really experience the imbalance. If you are in pain, it is your job to soothe or work through the pain on your side of the line. This may allow you to not experience pain with the imbalance, or it may compel you to problem solve with your partner to change the imbalance.

Here are some examples:
- Someone who is consistently forgetful or loses track of time would set a reminder and/or alarm in order to do a task, exit from their activity, or be on time. A partner who is often late would call or text their partner about their estimated arrival time or choose intentional behaviors to help them be on time.
- A couple in which one partner earns more money would discuss and make financial decisions together, have discretionary allowances, and decide on big expenditures in an I Count–You Count spirit of the agreement.
- A partner who exhibits consistent behaviors that cause pain to their partner would get evaluated for possible causes (depression, mood disorders, personality disorders, addictions, unresolved fatigue, highly anxious, frequent

illness, easily emotionally overwhelmed, unkind repetitive responses and behaviors).

- If your partner tells you that a behavior is creating worry, anxiety, or fear— believe them. This is in the spirit of the Equal Say So balance. Evaluate the situation and seek understanding and/or help and take responsibility for the behavior (shopping, food, over the counter drugs, recreational drugs, substances, activities, and relationships).
- If your partner is struggling and unhappy with extended family or mutual friends relationships—believe them. If you disagree with your partner, use the I Count–You Count Dialog to work the problem.

It bears repeating that if you are in an I Count–You Count relationship, if your partner tells you they are distressed or in pain about something, you believe them. You do what you can to work the problem. Likewise, if you are experiencing distress and pain because of your partner, it is your job to speak up, advocate, set boundaries, and protect yourself if necessary.

Each partnership must work out the commitment in their unique way. If each person of the partnership shows up with their side of the line and gives effort to the Win-Win, Contentment can be reached even if things are not perfect or fixed. The work of a relationship is to honor both sides of the line to the greatest extent possible.

If you feel that your side is not understood or not honored, it is your partnership duty to respectfully advocate for it. It is never an I Count–You Count to demand your partner make your side of the line better or demand something different from your partner's side of the line. Request, yes! Demand, no!

However, it is possible that when you honor your side of the line—your truth, your experience—you realize that the relationship is not an equal partnership. You realize it is not a healthy, Contented relationship. If a partner is not willing to honor your side of the relationship, is not willing to work on the foundation of I Count–You Count, and you honestly have done your best to fully partner, then it is your job to honor and protect your side of the line. It is possible that a relationship may not work—that one or both people cannot fully honor the spirit of the I Count–You Count agreement.

I Count—You Count Dialog

Me   You

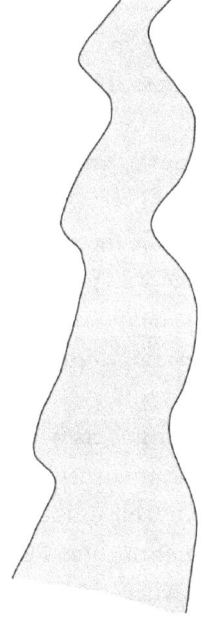

THOUGHTS	THOUGHTS
EMOTIONS, FEELINGS	EMOTIONS, FEELINGS
NEEDS	NEEDS
REQUESTS	REQUESTS
WANTS, DESIRES	WANTS, DESIRES
BODY EXPERIENCES, MESSAGES	BODY EXPERIENCES, MESSAGES
MY ISSUES, MY STUFF	MY ISSUES, MY STUFF

About the Yellow Light Encounters Exercises

Practicing the Yellow Light Encounters Exercises

The Yellow Light Encounter encourages couples to practice, prioritize, negotiate, and proactively take time to enjoy and make contact with one another. The metaphor of a stoplight is used to help the couple be verbally clear in their negotiations. Green light means "I am ready and want to have sex." Red light means "I do not want to have sex." The yellow light means "I want to be here with you and we'll see how it goes."

When we are driving our car and come upon an intersection with a yellow blinking light, we know to proceed with caution. Unlike the green light where we know we can cross and others must wait, the yellow light alerts us that we need to decide if it is safe to keep going. This metaphor is helpful in resetting problematic sex negotiations for a couple.

The main focus of this exercise is for a couple to practice prioritizing and inviting each other to a "Yellow Light Encounter."

The goal of each Yellow Light Encounter is to be present with your partner, including emotional presence and awareness, mental presence and awareness, and physical presence and awareness. Each Yellow Light is a success if both partners show up and do their best to be present with each other. As the couple progresses in their mutual full engagement, the exercises become more challenging and support the couple in their skillfulness in making bids for sexual contact.

A complete guide to the Yellow Light Encounters is offered in the Wise Sex Revive Master Class. The Wise Sex Revive Master Class is a program that helps couples revive, reset, and restart their sex life. Based on proven exercises used in sex therapy, the program guides you through phases that help you become progressively more skillful in your ability to be intimate, reconnect as partners, and overcome desire and sex issues. The Wise Sex Revive Master Class is offered by Sensovi Institute at Sensovi.com.

About the Sexual Experiences and Behavior Inventory (SEABI)

About the Sexual Experiences and Behavior Inventory (SEABI)

In the last chapter, "Graduation," Ted and Erica's results from their Sexual Experiences and Behavior Inventory (SEABI) were discussed. Here are some more details about the assessment.

We compared their SEABI diagrams that showed their sexual templates and their sexuality stories. The three main categories of the template are Arousal Focused, Emotional Regulation Focused, and Presence Focused.

Ted scored highest in Fantasy and Erotic Energy components, which are Arousal Focused. He also scored high on the Emotional Regulation component of Anonymous. In other words, the activities and experiences that Ted said he liked or would like to try were Arousal and Emotional Regulation focused.

Erica's highest three were Erotic Energy (Arousal Focused), Power Affirmation, and Barter (both are Emotional Regulation focused).

Both Ted and Erica scored very low on Presence Focused sections. Neither Ted nor Erica answered that they liked or would like to try very many of the Presence Focused questions. For example, "I have a heightened sense of my whole body when I am having sex," or "My partner and I give each other verbal feedback during sex." Their templates confirmed that after the initial wake up arousal, they both "dozed off to sleep" and went wherever their Rivers took their Body Boats. In other words, they did not have an open Intimacy Bridge and they did not partner in building one.

The SEABI is an online assessment that offers an in-depth understanding of your Relationship and Intimacy skills and Sexuality template. Developed and refined from relationship and sex therapy principles, you are provided with a written report and visual graph of your unique template, along with suggestions for resources to meet your personal goals. Whether you want a healthier relationship or better sex life, understanding the "You Are Here" place in the map of your life provided by the SEABI can help you be successful. The SEABI is offered by Sensovi Institute at Sensovi.com.

Acknowledgments

I want to express my gratitude for everyone who supported me in the work and birthing of this book.

I acknowledge and thank my clients for trusting and entrusting me with their stories and their journeys to find Contentment. Many times, we have learned together, and at times you have shown me how to open my heart to my own not knowing what I don't know. Many have shared with me exercise and handout refinements, language suggestions, and read the earliest drafts. Thank you.

Ideas and definitions of Self and Happiness are in no short supply. Many books, researchers, professors, talk shows, blogs, YouTubers, and podcasts abound. I know because I have stacks of books and a huge list of podcasts. In this vast sea of words and ideas, my vision statement, "to alleviate suffering in relationships and sexuality," keeps me clear on the idea that I will always need to paddle through the many rivers of ideas and knowledge to effectively help my clients.

I acknowledge and thank those who have come before me and walk beside me in this work. I want to acknowledge that if there is something in this book that inspires or helps you, the reader, I was able to share it with you "while standing on the shoulders of giants." It was because others came before me and many continue to carry the work forward.

Kathy, I am so grateful for lovely you—and you win! Even from Bundaberg, you managed to be there for me when this book was just a vision. You traveled the furthest of anyone both metaphorically and literally in your support of my vision for this book over the years it has taken to finish it. Thank you.

Thank you, Afra, my beautiful, steady, and gentle nurse friend. Our breakfast get-togethers, your listening ear and sharing were a lifeline to me, especially during the height of Covid and working in a crumbling, stressful hospital culture. And just like I hear everyone say, I love Afra too!

Marlea, my sweet colleague and beautiful friend. You give such good gifts, especially the gift of helping me feel seen and heard, and always making me feel that you believed I would finish this supposed book. Thank you.

Lynne, my lovely and energetic friend. We have been friends through many years of bonfires, art making, cats, woodland critters, chicken tacos, projects, walks, and talks. I always know that when either you or I go "m.i.a.," we will eventually be walking the prairie together again even if we have to use canes to do it. Thank you.

Becky, my lovely and early Sensovi friend. Thank you for your very patient listening ear through the years and your delight in chocolate sundaes. Our times together supported me both through good times and challenging times. Thank you.

David, your salon chair, your music, your attentiveness and compassion, and our big picture conversations always lifted me back to my hopes for this book. Each haircut appointment energized and renewed me to my intentions. Thank you.

Carrie, my lovely Pitta hiking buddy. Thank you for your willingness to go "there" and talk about "that" with me. I treasure our discussions.

Tonya, my big-hearted, lovely, and loyal sister. You read my very first unpublished "book" and remembered it—as only a sister can do—when I had forgotten about it. I know I can call you at any time and you will go camping, or floating, and you will have my back. Thank you. I love you, sister!

Joshua, thank you for your helpful feedback and willingness to workshop my book ideas, and the many times you checked in on how it was going. I love you, son.

Micah, our many discussions about being present and awake, you checking in about the book, and your insightful feedback on the manuscript got me over the finish line. Thank you. I love you, son.

Rick, I love you.

About the Author

Dr. Lisa Terrell is a Licensed Clinical Mental Health Counselor and Certified Sex Therapist and Sexologist. She has a Relationship- and Sexuality-focused private practice in Charlotte, North Carolina.

In 2007, she founded Sensovi Institute, an online campus that offers classes, assessments, remedial programs, and resources for relationships and sex-related issues. She is the author of *Snow People World: Healthy and Happy Relationships* and the Wise Self Workshops. The Wise Self Workshops are available at Sensovi.com

Also By Author

Snowpeople World: Happy and Healthy Relationships Amazon.com

Wise Self Workshops and Assessments. Online programs for relationship and sex therapy, including the Wise Self Sex Revive Masterclass and the Sexual Experiences and Behavior Inventory (SEABI). Sensovi.com